THE
SILENT CIRCLES
OF TRUTH

SHURA GEHRMAN

THE
SILENT CIRCLES
OF TRUTH

With an Introduction by
Colin Wilson

André Deutsch

First published in Great Britain in 1995 by
André Deutsch Limited
106 Great Russell Street
London WC1B 3LJ

ISBN 0 233 98910 2

Design by Jeffrey Sains
Typeset by Falcon Graphic Art Ltd.

Cataloguing-in-Publication data available for this title
from the British Library

Printed in Singapore

Contents

List of Illustrations

28. August 1993, pastel and acrylic, 29.6 × 26.6cm.
29. August 1993, ink and pastel on paper, 30.1 × 39.2cm.
30. August 1993, pastel and ink on paper, 29.8 × 38.6cm.
31. 1993, acrylic and pastel on paper, 29.2 × 38.5cm.
32. 'The two Shuras' (artist unknown), watercolour on ivory, 6.5 × 10cm.

BLACK AND WHITE:
  1. 1993, pastel on paper, 24.6 × 19.8cm.
  2. 2 September 1993, ink on paper, 29.1 × 20.3cm.
  3. 4.17am 24 November 1993, ink and pastel on paper, 40.5 × 29.2cm.
  4. October 1993, ink on paper, 14.8 × 10.5cm.
  5. October 1993, ink on paper, 25 × 19.8cm.
  6. September 1993, ink on paper, 24.6 × 19.1cm.
  7. January 1994, ink on paper, 24.7 × 19.3cm.
  8. September 1993, ink on paper, 28.7 × 19.7cm.
  9. September 1993, ink and acrylic on paper, 29.2 × 20.5cm.
10. September 1993, ink on paper, 29.1 × 20.4cm.
11. November 1993, ink on paper, 24.4 × 19.9cm.
12. July 1993, charcoal and pastel on paper, 20.2 × 14.2cm.
13. July 1993, pencil on paper, 20.3 × 14.2cm.
14. 21 August 1993, pastel and ink on paper, 29.1 × 20.4cm.
15. July 1993, acrylic and pastel on paper, 40.5 × 29.2cm.
16. August 1993, ink on paper, 24.9 × 19.1cm.
17. September 1993, ink on paper, 24.7 × 19.1cm.
18. September 1993, ink on paper, 25.8 × 35.5cm.
19. October 1993, ink on paper, 24.1 × 20cm.
20. 1 September 1993, ink on paper, 13.2 × 17.1cm.
21. August 1993, ink on paper, 13.2 × 17.1cm.
22. July 1993, charcoal on paper, 39 × 28.6cm.
23. October 1993, ink on paper, 23.4 × 20cm.
24. 4.00pm August 1993, ink and pencil on paper, 40 × 29.3cm.
25. November 1993, ink and charcoal on paper, 39.9 × 29.2cm.
26. October 1993, ink on paper, 24.5 × 19.8cm.
27. September 1993, ink on paper, 39.2 × 29.8cm.
28. September 1993, ink on paper, 16.5 × 19.5cm.
29. August 1993, ink on paper, 24.8 × 17.3cm.
30. July 1993, charcoal and pastel on paper, 29.1 × 20.4cm.
31. 1993, ink and pastel on paper, 13.9 × 10.9cm.
32. November 1993, ink on paper, 14 × 10.1cm.

Introduction by Colin Wilson

'The name of Shura Gehrman meant nothing to me when I was asked to review a boxed set of four records . . . After two minutes, however, my ears pricked up, and some three hours later I realised that I had experienced something which I can only describe as a revelation . . .' It was these words, in a review by Frank Granville Barker in *Records and Recording*, that sent me hurrying out to buy the boxed set entitled 'German and French Songs'. But I must admit that I was also intrigued by a strikingly hostile review by Andrew Keener in *Hi Fi News*, in which he speaks of 'a vocal quality of unwieldy, even sinister character', and ends by admitting that he is at a loss for a musical rating because the singer had obviously achieved all he set out to do. If critics could disagree so completely, it seemed to indicate that Gehrman was at least a singer of considerable individuality.

I had been fascinated by the art of singing ever since, in my mid-teens, a friend had spent whole evenings playing me old 78s of great opera singers – Caruso, Chaliapin, Plancon, Tamagno, Melba, Lily Pons, and comparing their techniques. As soon as my first book made me enough money to be able to afford records, I began to collect them. Among these early acquisitions was the old American Rococo set of Reynaldo Hahn, Proust's intimate friend and the composer of the delightful *Ciboulette*. I came to love these recordings; like the paintings of the Impressionists and the stories of Maupassant, they seemed to encapsulate the life of a whole epoch.

So when the Shura Gehrman songs arrived, it was natural that the first record I played should be the one of Fauré and Gounod songs. Instantly, I found myself enveloped in the familiar magic; I can remember giving a sigh of contentment and relaxing as if in a warm bath. Gehrman's voice was a far more powerful instrument than Hahn's (one could say of Hahn, without disparagement, that he was a drawing-room tenor), and he was, of course, a baritone; but there was indisputably much of the same quality. The first word that occurred to me as I listened to these performances was 'virile'. But I suppose that what struck me most was that the experience of listening to his voice was far more like the experience of listening to some of the great singers of the past rather than to modern singers I admired – Fischer-Dieskau, Hermann Prey, Alexander Young, Wilfred Brown.

I could also understand what Andrew Keener meant when he said: 'at full tilt Mr Gehrman's voice is a fearsome, clarion-like instrument, bearing down on a phrase with doom-laden menace.' Yet for me, this was also an integral part of the performances; if Gehrman had a voice of such power, it seemed absurd not to use it.

The modern world has become accustomed to an extremely high degree of technical virtuosity in its singers and instrumentalists, and this has become accompanied by a tendency to coolness and restraint. But this can occasionally produce the impression that Roy Campbell complained about in speaking of certain South African novelists:

> You praise the firm restraint with which they write –
> I'm with you there, of course.
> They use the snaffle and the curb alright,
> But where's the bloody horse?

The result is that – for example – most modern pianists can play the Beethoven sonatas better than Schnabel – certainly without the profusion of wrong notes; yet none of them can equal Schnabel in power and imaginative insight.

It took me only five minutes to recognise that Gehrman, like Schnabel, is a 'romantic', and that when he sings Fauré or Schubert, he does it somehow from 'inside', as if he had become identified with the composer. This is what the critic Roger Nichols meant when he wrote: 'the great strength of Gehrman's art is that he not only soars above the limits of the genteel, but plunges below the surface of the words to the deeper meanings . . .' Certainly, 'genteel' was the last word anyone would associate with Gehrman.

It was only later that I discovered that Gehrman was the founder and President of Nimbus Records, and that his real name was Count Numa Labinsky. He kept his identity a secret for the obvious reason: because he did not want hostile critics accusing him of founding a record company merely in order to issue his own recordings. In fact,

2

Gehrman had originally founded the recording company twenty-seven years earlier, in 1957, and had refused to make any recordings until 1972.

I made contact with Gehrman, and not long after, in July 1984, there was an overpowering racket in the sky above our house in Cornwall, and Adrian Farmer and Shura Gehrman emerged from a helicopter. It was typical of him to take a helicopter – as another man might take a taxi – to drop in for lunch.

Shura was a small, bearded man who reminded me of photographs of D H Lawrence. He also had the quality described so often by Lawrence's friends: a kind of vital warmth that seemed to flow naturally from him. Most people seem 'closed in', as if they are interposing a barrier between themselves and other people; Shura was like his singing: completely 'open'.

Physically speaking, he was rather frail; he had experienced a great deal of illness, and when we went out to lunch – at a nearby vineyard – he ate and drank almost nothing. But he was plainly a man of enormous nervous energy. And there was something about this contrast between his physical frailty and his nervous energy that intrigued me. My first impressions of him confirmed what I had guessed from his records, and from some of the poetry he had sent me: that here was a man born out of his time. He seemed to belong to the nineteenth rather than the twentieth century, to the age of romanticism. He would have felt totally at home in that little dining club that used to meet at Magny's, in the Rue Mazet in Paris, in the 1860s, and whose members included Flaubert, Sainte-Beuve, the Goncourt brothers and Theophile Gautier. His poetry, like his conversation, revealed a Proustian sensibility, an alertness to shades of meaning combined with intellectual precision. Yet it soon became clear that my attempt to classify him as a 'romantic outsider' was an oversimplification; there was a steely element about him that made him quite unlike the many romantic outsiders I have known. And the exact nature of the difference suddenly crystallised when we were speaking about his father, a Russian nobleman who had fled to France at the time of the Revolution. He remarked that his father was not a weak man, but that he was a sad man, who always dreamed of returning to Russia. Then he added meditatively: 'My father – I think – was a born loser, as I am a born winner.'

I found this an extremely interesting realisation. For this had been the problem at the heart of my first book, *The Outsider*. The outsider-romantics experienced moods of almost mystical ecstasy, in which they felt that life is full of infinite potentialities. Then they woke up the next morning and felt once again 'stranded' in a world that seemed too harsh, too real. And they felt that they had to pay for the moods of ecstasy and mystical affirmation with a certain inability to cope with everyday life, a certain shrinking incompetence. This is why so many of them committed suicide, or died of wasting illnesses. The existentialists – who followed the romantics – were slightly more cheerful. Hemingway once said: 'A man can be destroyed but not defeated.' But they still felt that life is fundamentally tragic and futile. In *The Outsider*, I pointed out that most of the romantics were defeated by self-pity rather than by a tragic destiny; the basic message of the book was that the Outsider should be capable of being a winner rather than a loser. He merely has to decide that he has no intention of being either destroyed or defeated. Shura was the first person I had met who seemed to conform to this pattern of what I thought of as the 'post-existentialist outsider'.

Shura has told me of the traumatic effect on him of the death, at the age of seven, of his twin brother. Shura's reaction was twofold. He began to sing, sitting for hours on top of the stairs, making wordless crooning sounds. And he turned his back on the world of actuality – even to the extent of standing for hours facing a blank wall – and lived in a fantasy world in which his twin was still alive.

Most of us have tried to do something of the sort, to compensate for the unsatisfactoriness of the real world – and no doubt most of us have found the exercise thoroughly unsatisfying. But Shura had certain advantages: the singlemindedness of a child, and the sheer intensity of the relationship with his dead twin. There was also the fact that he lacked emotional compensations in the adult world that surrounded him. His father was a detached, abstracted sort of person; his mother was a practical and dominant Frenchwoman; Shura felt no close attachment to either. So the fantasy world, in which his brother was still alive, became reality.

In describing this to me, he used the interesting phrase 'going into free fall'. It intrigued me because at the time, I had just finished writing a book about Jung, and Jung had described a similar experience. It had happened in a time of great mental stress, just after the break with Freud, when Jung was afraid that he was going insane. One day, as he sat at his desk struggling against depression, he suddenly decided to 'let go'. 'I let myself drop. Suddenly it was as though the ground literally gave way beneath my feet and I plunged into dark depths. But then, abruptly,

4

at not too great a depth, I landed on my feet in a soft, sticky mess.' He found himself in a cave, guarded by a dwarf, then saw a stream in which the body of a blond youth was floating. Jung had learned to dream with his eyes open, creating an inner world of imagination with such vividness that it became totally real. From then on, he was always able to gain access to this state that he called 'active imagination'. It seems clear that Shura learned the same trick when his twin died – and did not entirely lose it.

Shura has written: 'The legacy (my brother) left me was the knowledge of the need to love. When that idea formed itself in my mind there was a conflict with myself. How could I love again? It was then that I realised that loving has a beginning *and an ending*. First this was unacceptable; the hurt of loss was too much, I thought. But the alternative I knew to be impossible as well. So in the nightmare of loss I decided to want to love – and to be able to love other people; and so my search started then.'

This could have been the formula for creating an emotional cripple; in fact, he was saved by his peculiar blend of toughness and imagination. That strange ability to go into a state of 'free fall' made him aware of meanings that were hidden from other people. On the walks – which he now took alone – he experienced again and again the curious sense that material objects were communicating with him. He found that he could listen to the sound of a stream, or stare at a crumbling stone wall, and experience an oddly satisfying sense of meaning. This was not imagination; it was what Gottfried Benn calls 'primal perception', the simple, clear perception of the intuitions, before the 'old mill of the mind' has had time to dilute their immediacy. He experienced the same sensation when his family took him to the seaside, staring with a perfect contentment at the sea, as if its rhythms were a form of speech.

Yet a point came – he estimates that it was in his fourteenth year – when his inborn will to health triumphed over the feelings of world-rejection. He says that he finally recognised that the tendency to lose himself in the world of imagination could only lead to increased withdrawal from reality, and perhaps finally to insanity. This insight seems to have corresponded roughly with the end of childhood and the beginning of puberty. Whatever the reason, it seems that he suddenly decided to break the habit of retreating into a state of 'free fall'. His character was a blend of Slavic romanticism, derived from his father, and a determined pragmatism, inherited from his mother. Now, fortunately for his health and sanity, the pragmatism won the day.

In the original version of this Introduction, written for a privately printed edition of his poems in 1988, I had gone on: 'This is not the place to describe his remarkable life, from the time when, at fifteen, he hitch-hiked across Europe, through to the founding of Nimbus; all this must be the subject of his autobiography, already part written.'

In fact, the autobiography, called *Time Remembered*, was still only a fragment at the time of his death – of a stroke – on 28 January 1994, in his sixty-ninth year. In spite of all my attempts to persuade him to finish it, he abandoned it because, he said, he found these attempts to recall his own past too traumatic. It is here printed for the first time.

I suspect it may have been this determination to turn his back on the past that led him to the incredible burst of activity that continued throughout the 1980s, and which seemed to prove that, no matter how unwilling the flesh may be, it can always be driven to obey sheer willpower. Shura not only continued to be active in the running of Nimbus, but also engaged in a number of personal projects: singing, recording, forming a drama company (one of whose projects was to record Proust's vast novel) and designing and building a concert hall. He wanted to turn Wyastone Leys into an Aldeburgh or Glyndebourne, and when the concert hall was opened by the Prince of Wales in 1993, seemed well on his way to doing so. Nimbus also built a factory on the other side of the Atlantic, and at one point went into partnership with Robert Maxwell – whom Shura liked but distrusted, and which was to become a source of some regret.

Shura kept me informed of all these developments by telephone, usually talking for not less than half an hour. I detest the telephone, and Shura was the only friend whom I made no attempt to discourage from using the infuriating instrument; this was partly because I knew he hated letter writing, but largely because his calls were so amusing and outrageous that I relished them as dramatic performances. He once spent nearly an hour on the telephone from the South of France, at the 'peak period' of the day; this was not extravagance so much as part of his general desire to emphasise that he didn't give a damn for the kind of considerations that other people regard as important. In fact, I would say that this was the salient trait of his personality, which he often carried to extremes. (He told me how, when someone he had invited to lunch suggested that he was Jewish, he disproved the point by unzipping his fly and exposing himself.)

It must be admitted that he took pleasure in playing the *enfant terrible*, and his quoted opinions were often so outrageous that they

6

created a dangerously inaccurate impression of wilfulness and frivolity. But while it is true that Shura had the spontaneity and unpredictability of a hyperactive child, this masked an obsessive conviction that the arts are essential to civilised values, and that a society that neglects its art is unconsciously preparing itself for its own extinction. In this sense, he was one of the most serious men I have ever known.

He proved the point again less than six months before his death. In September 1993, with a box of French crayons, he suddenly began producing extraordinary pictures. He sent me some of the first, and I was astounded at their quality. Some of them might be unknown drawings by Egon Schiele; some of the faces (he called them 'masks') have the frightening power of Schoenberg's expressionistic self-portraits. In five weeks he poured out fifty of these remarkable sketches and watercolours, leaving no doubt whatever that he could, if he had wished, have made a career as an artist. I have photographs of these pictures on my desk as I write, and as I look at them I realise once more that Shura was an incredibly gifted man who possessed many of the virtues – and some of the faults – of a great artist.

When I asked him if he had ever had any thought of becoming an artist, he said that he hadn't, but *had* once received some encouragement in that direction. When he was twenty, he and his mother had moved into a cottage in the South of France. One day, as he was lying on the white sands of the beach twenty miles away, he suddenly smelt the distinctive odour of bouillabaisse, and followed his nose into some nearby woods, where he found a large and rather fat artist in the garden of a small cottage. Shura knew he was an artist because he was drawing on a canvas – which stood on an easel – with a crayon which was attached to a five foot twig. Typically, Shura walked into the garden uninvited and got into conversation with the man, who introduced himself as Henri Matisse, a name that meant nothing to Shura. But they took a liking to one another, and Shura was invited into the cottage to share the bouillabaisse. Matisse told him that he was at present obliged to cook for himself because his wife had just walked out, and the young girl who usually did the housework had been forced to leave, on account of local gossip to the effect that she was his mistress. 'And was she?' asked Shura, and Matisse confessed that this had been his intention. He added that he found young girls sexually exciting, and that, as an artist, he felt he had every right to his enthusiasms. Shura told him he was a dirty old pig, and Matisse cheerfully agreed.

Whenever he and his mother went to the beach, Shura called in on his new acquaintance, having no idea that he was one of the most celebrated artists in Europe. Matisse handed him crayons and encouraged him to draw, telling him that he had talent. But Shura already felt that his talent lay in singing, and had no intention of following Matisse's advice. When he and his mother left soon after, he lost touch with his genial and eccentric friend.

Shelley once called poets 'the unacknowledged legislators of the world.' But what Shura means when he speaks of the poet as a kind of Promethean goes even further than that. He was in the unique position of a 'romantic outsider' who was also an inventor and a successful business man, so that he recognised that the creative force that produces poetry is not fundamentally different in kind from the creative force that produces science, or even creates a business. Shakespeare knows that the poet's imagination 'bodies forth the forms of things unknown', and give to airy nothings 'a local habitation and a name.' But when a pioneer builds a log cabin, when a scientist thinks of a new use for the binary code, he is doing precisely the same thing. So there is a very real sense in which our civilisation is a creation of the imagination. It is a poetic creation, in the same sense as the *Odyssey* or the *Divine Comedy*. This is what Shura means when he says that the poet is responsible for humanity, even every animal that lives, and why he called one of his Schubert records 'The Man Who Steals the Flame', and another, 'Eyes to a Distant Horizon'.

We live in a pessimistic culture, where most of our distinguished Nobel Prize winners are people who believe that the basic truth of human life is cruelty, betrayal and futility. If Gehrman is right – and I believe he is – this in itself is enough to explain why we appear to be living in a 'dying culture' whose prevailing atmosphere is one of defeat. This recognition forms the background of his assertion: 'The poet would measure the awakening of all the unknown in the universal noosphere of his own time, building on past words a bridge to the future time . . .'

Yet his poetry is not, in itself, abstract or 'idealistic'; it is as completely personal as that of Cavafy. I first understood what poetry meant to him when I encouraged him to write autobiography, and observed with bafflement the immense effort of personal agony that it cost him. This was not, I think, entirely because he was trying to exorcise many painful memories. It was also because telling the story of his past life lacked immediacy. His poems are what Joyce called 'epiphanies', snapshots of moments of intense reality. They capture the essence of his

8

life as it was actually lived; by comparison, autobiography must seem a distant, abstract mode of expression. These poems could not have been written but for that long period of 'inwardness' during his childhood, and that curious ability he learned to relax in a world of 'free fall'. At their worst, they may seem like aphorisms or reflections. At their best, they are mirror-like fragments of a mind that reflects reality.

Time Remembered

The house trembles
  and the dust leaves of memory vanish into the forgotten land,
The door opens
  and the shaken world returns.
Unload all impersonal outward observances
  and take up your burdens
    that bring sorrow after the easy crying is past.
The road is black with mourning.

Sometimes the things which one is purposefully shocked into forgetting when young now return clearly to mind. The voice which is speaking these pains is my own. To be at last able to expel the greatest hurt which has lain dormant in the mind – to know that somehow I may speak of Shura 1 and Shura 2, is utterly surprising.

We were identical twins, and for the first year of our lives, from the time we were born until we were two years old, I have no recollection whatsoever of our sameness. Then I remember the table with a cake which had two candles on its white surface. It was decorated with sugared almonds round the edge, and there was also a straight line of them which seemed to divide the one cake into two. Shura, my twin, was standing at one end of the room and I at the other. We were facing each other, looking, it seemed, into a mirror which reflected an identical image. So at that moment in time we knew that we loved each other. We did not speak, because we became aware quite harshly and quite miraculously that we belonged to each other.

So it began, this huge mystery of being aware of myself in my brother. More and more we became inseparable; we also became the curiosity of our family. We were, as it were, the star turn. We on our part did not enjoy this development, now I am able to look back on it; we sought to enclose ourselves away from as much of this as possible. We did not seem to need any other companionship. By thinking, by going into free fall, we invented a silent language for ourselves which we understood. Any language spoken to us then came as a sudden shock, an intrusion; we sensed the danger from our family rather quickly, sometimes days, sometimes minutes before it arrived. We knew or sensed when our people were in anger, apathy, pain or love. There were very sudden moves of mood and temper – this was strange to us, for we were locked into a firm contentment of our being, and acted rather as we were expected to behave towards the other world and as that world wished us to behave. So we learnt to behave thus; from this strange world we seemed removed.

There was, however, one man we loved to be with, my father's great friend, Vassily Kousnitsov – Russian, tall, blond. We always asked to be told stories. He would start by lifting us up and kissing us on our heads. Then he would begin, always in the same way: 'There was a treasure in the mind of the blind girl, as you have your treasure in each other.' Thus we fell in love with him, the only other person in our lives that mattered.

I remember my grandmother taking us on a holiday to Blankenburg, the white sands seemingly endless to us, and we would walk for a long time, our heads down, looking at the very few stones which were embedded like large pearls. There were sand dunes which attracted us, and there the sand was much softer to our feet. The house which she rented every year in late summer for six weeks was simple, clean, tidy. We used to get up at six each morning. Gogo, our grandmother, was French; she was preparing our breakfast, which consisted of large bowls of very hot black sweet coffee and nearly white creamy-looking salted butter which we loved to spread thickly on our freshly-baked bread. No words, but our silent dialogue continued. '*Les salles Russes,*' she always muttered before crossing herself and lapsing into silence for a moment as she said her Hail Marys and Our Fathers twice through, always looking at us with some misgiving. When she had finished praying, she would ask us the same question every day: 'Now tell me, what are you two telling each other? It's not natural, no, not natural that you seem never to have to talk to each other like that. It's as though you can understand each other somehow. No, it's not natural at all.' There was no answer to her cross-questioning us, so we remained silent for a while. Then Shura would say to her simply, 'Have you slept well, Gogo?' The reply, snorted out, was always the same: 'When you grow old, sleep is not much with you. When you grow old, you'll see, when it's your turn.'

Other people of our age did not seem in any way wanted. They puzzled us because they shouted so often. We could not understand their needs, and indeed what seemed to please them was rather mysterious to us – skipping, playing, tumbling, falling, throwing, destroying. Their pastimes were not interesting to us. Perhaps we were never children, or perhaps our games were so different that they and we could never find a bridge to cross over for any meeting between us. To one and to both, our games were invisible; a type of searching, a type of understanding without knowing.

10

So we became four years old, and our loving increased. There was no measurement of time in our minds then. I remember that in our fifth year you, my brother, suddenly spoke out aloud to me. The strange beauty of your speech made me answer in the same way, although to me my voice did not sound like yours. 'Shura,' you said, 'we shall become afraid to lose us.' I wept, and was awake to the fact that although we were one person, in reality there were two of us and that I wanted so much never to be separated from my brother. This was the time of my first knowledge of fear, of unsettlement in the pivot and harbour of my life. I became more afraid of losing him.

Our simple toys were stones and small rock fossils, which held a deep interest for us. Somehow we felt familiar in our minds that they belonged to us, and also that we belonged with water, in clear brooks and streams.

And so our years together passed. We became ill; I cannot remember the illness which made us feverish and full of spots, even in our mouths. Then, for the very first time, we were quite unable to communicate without speaking aloud. This frightened us, but, as we began to recover, the speaking aloud became less and less necessary. We continued our silent dialogue and became one again. But we became aware paradoxically that we were each half of the other's being.

Now that I am a grown man and look at children of four and five years old, I marvel, and sometimes wonder if I have remembered our early years together in order of truth; then the certainty of these things which befell the two of us becomes stronger again. I remember his hair, his fingernails and the solemn looks of expression; and the last, more than any other, his very deep brown eyes. If you are able to see and by misfortune go blind, you are always able to remember colours, shapes, and all the things which you have in your first years of sight become accustomed to; so do I remember them clearly.

As our last year came upon us, I think everything started as before. I remember that our mother and father decided to go to Bavaria at Christmas-time, thus leaving us with a household of only ten adults, including, of course, our grandmother Gogo, her sister Matante, my mother's old nurse with her husband who looked after the gardens and the *potager*, the vegetable garden, who became madder and madder, inventing people who would most surely kill him. He always referred to them as the *'Du Moulins'*; he would suddenly charge out of the outhouses with his pitchfork, stabbing the nearest tree, which when done would seem to satisfy his delusions, and disappearing into his workshop quite contentedly, and calm would return to the household, the chickens slowly getting over their havoc and hysteria. The cats and dogs never seemed affected by him (although I do remember that they never became friendly towards *mon oncle* Achile) – to us they seemed the wisest creatures of the entire ménage.

The Aunts by that time would be praying, their beads working overtime on Hail Marys and Our Fathers. All ills were thus treated. Both of them, my grandmother and her sister, were completely captivated by my father, to them charming and without fault. My twin and I felt only curiosity for him. We neither liked, loved nor disliked him. He distanced himself I think from us – and we returned the same echo of distance to him. We felt his interest in us to be nil and nothing breeds nothing. He dreamt of the ballet and of large country estates, fast motor cars and his many friends in the arts and theatre. He smoked heavy Russian cigarettes through a shagreen holder incessantly, waiting, always waiting, for the return, the return to Russia! My father always thought up things which would make him very rich indeed. He had taken us on holiday to the white sands of the Belgian Coast, in the twenties and early thirties completely empty, wonderfully cheap. Great aunts, new young maids (always from the country, always giggling), trunk loads of baggage, my mother's dogs and my parrot, all this nightmare of travel somehow managed, after following my father who led the way with his great friend Vassily sitting next to him, pleading with him not to be so reckless in driving the very large motor car that he had not paid for, or for that matter never could, or would. The retinues arrived by car and train in various stages of bad temper and exhaustion. He always had a new person that was going to make a fortune for him, his family and the world. Where those dreadful people came from only my father could have known. Blankenburg then had one splendid hotel. My father had asked for an entire floor for his entourage, that he would require a man servant immediately, complete room service, telephones – the lot. That he was not to be disturbed by anyone on any account. He had much too much to do in this starving and depressing world. His new venture was to be a vast string of bakers' shops throughout England – because the people always needed bread – and next door there would be radio wireless shops, the new entertainment for the people. My father's ideas always had a core of truth, he trusted everyone and seemed completely sure of himself. So convincing was he that he thought of himself as able to undertake business enterprises of this order. It ended sadly because there was no one able to stop him, to tell him that he was an innocent fool

12

in matters of business, though never dishonest. For him it was always a game.

We, as observers, could accept all we saw – not ever thinking that this behaviour was in any way strange. While my father went from one scheme to another without the slightest problem, the managers would see to whatever problems there were. My mother and her family were French and always picked up the broken pieces of my father's shattered dreams.

My mother, being highly volatile (but very fond of roses, indeed of all flowers), was not I think happy because she was quite unable to cope with my father, his friends, his thoughts and his way of life. She was used to harvesting and the seasons, the earth and its growing of crops and of her most beloved roses. This hurts me to write, this remembrance always comes sadly.

My grandmother was not interested very much in her daughter's 'flower madness' as she termed it. She, Gogo, was the housekeeper – the linen sheets, the soap, the hawk eyes of order, the dread of the young maids fresh from their homes never ever cleaning well enough to please her. Nothing was ever done well enough. Order and warmth were her main preoccupations and she was satisfied that her sister, whom she loved more than any other person, was not unwell. She, my great aunt, never complained. In fact she was the kindest person I have known, a complete person. I never remember her eating with us, or her eating anything other than bread and her only drink was milk. She also loved my dog Mimie. She suffered very probably in many ways although no one ever heard her complain. She rose from bed at 5.30 am and was about her duties in the kitchens and laundry before anyone else. We never realised that she had become blind until she had fallen headlong down some rather steep stone stairs and had hit her head on a radiator which was at the foot of the steps. This fragment comes out of time, out of context – now memory slips back to other times, trying, replacing.

My father's small retinue, all Russian of course, would remain quite aloof from 'all this vulgarity', as they referred to my mother's side of the family, who were fully aware that speaking in Russian meant something disparaging was being said about them.

All this of course was observed by the two of us without much interest. We carried on in our private lives, learning most of the time by observing ourselves. There were of course intrusions into our two lives, and presents at quite unexpected times. Our parents gave us two cockatoos that year which pleased us a lot. In retrospect I think we loved our two dogs more than any of the other animals around us, who in turn loved us as much as we loved them. Our bedroom was large, with a boxroom adjoining it. It had shelves which held our toys, a few books, many, many stones and rocks, and a crystal set with two pairs of headphones; also our clothes. From the age of three, we had been told that in future we must make our own beds and clean our own shoes.

Our instruction was given us by the Jesuit Fathers and, to be fair, it interested the two of us greatly. We were taught the Catholic dogmas of course, most of which meant little to us. The Immaculate Conception seemed very puzzling, so of course we questioned it. We knew about the facts of life! Living in the country one saw the inevitable cows and bulls, dogs, bitches, cats, and even chickens having immaculate conceptions, or so we thought. But no, these were not at all the same thing, we were told quite severely. Nevertheless we asked if it was only human beings that had immaculate conceptions, which brought down great wrath and annoyance from our holy teacher. If God, we said to him, wanted to become a man, why did he not have to go and do the same as man himself? This terrible heresy was not acceptable to our teacher and caused the two of us much trouble and much soreness on our behinds. The more we questioned, the more cross they became with us. We were not very troubled, it did not seem important, nor could we relate to it ourselves, so I suppose we dismissed it altogether.

Our inner dialogue continued and our love for each other increased, and I cannot say that we were not becoming aware of our sexuality, or that we did not explore our bodies without a great deal of pleasure sometimes. But this we found was only a passing interest. It was much more important that the interior thoughts which we shared between us protected the two of us from the stupidity, the rituals and the silliness of the world outside.

On our birthday, the seventh birthday, my brother Shura died from diphtheria which both of us had contracted.

I lived, but my brother died. I no longer weep for him or, for that matter, for myself. 'A great desire awakes and grows until forgetfulness of thee.'

I saw the white coffin take you away. It seemed so small. They gave you a crucifix, put your hands upon your chest holding the cross, and your eyes closed, and I became one, or rather half of one. I could not do anything, or speak to members of my family. I felt emptied and hollow, and the silence of the mind became awesome. Before, when my brother was living, there was not the empty silence which I now became aware of. He had left me, and I wept, but not with tears. I really was alone for the first time in my life.

I can only write about what I have undergone and known, my joys, my sadness, my living. Oh yes I have cried like the whole world has cried and is still crying over now. But this is only an account of one person, or perhaps more properly half of a person, or so I have felt it to be because of my brother's death, which angered and hurt, hurts me still. All in the past. But it was my first loving, so although I have loved others since, probably more as I became older, it was that first knowing of love that awakened the centre of my existence.

But how to start, or where to start is troublesome. I remember that I felt quite alone after my brother's death. I remember one morning walking into my mother's linen room. There was a large table in the centre of it, a sewing machine, and the far wall had shelves which held bales of cloth. The window was tall and narrow and as I wound the metal shutter down, the sun seemed to fall into the room very brightly, picking out the flecks of dust and as I watched these dust particles become iridescent, the room fell away and I was completely joyful to become strangely part of this change, these colours. For the first time I felt an awareness that I was not alone or even myself any more. That I was being fed wordlessly with an insight of joy in knowing somehow that I was able to feel intensely and to transmit by some form or other this intense excitement and commitment which I felt towards others, and then I understood that loving and expressing to others this love would be the whole, the core of my living, no matter what I did in the coming future.

> You will not come back again.
> I shall forget nothing we shared.

With my brother alive we seemed complete. After his death, and the departure of Vassily Kousnitsov, I was unable to make any contact with my family whatsoever. Becoming wary of loving anyone at all, I sang more and more.

The seasons flowed on. My grandmother died when I was twelve. This, her dying, did not affect me very much, although she had tried to comfort me in my grief over my brother's death. The strange thing was that after my twin was dead no one in my family mentioned his name or referred to him again. On the other side, my side, I recreated him in my sad mind and continued to live in my memory with him. Brother mine, in my imagination he was still with me, and the sands of time did not make my sadness diminish. Walking along the same paths, in the same fields, I tried to reach him somehow, but the more I tried the more still and silent my mind became. I was lost.

Once the smell and resonance of Shura my brother seemed to recreate itself for me. There was no shape, no form, simply his presence remembered. The earth in the field which had been freshly cut by men's scythes, leaving only stubble ends of the crop of barley, brought home to me the fact that my one loving was gone for ever. I think that it was then that somehow my brother, or his remembered eyes, did wipe out my emptiness of spirit; the moment when I could smell the earth and the scents of the fruits of the earth had become real to me once more. In that moment, I knew that I would survive his dying.

The legacy that he left me was the knowledge of the need to love. When that idea formed itself in my mind it caused a conflict within me. How could I love again? It was then that I realised loving had a beginning and an ending. At first this was unacceptable: the hurt of loss was much too much, I thought. But the alternative I knew to be impossible as well. So in the nightmare of loss I decided to want to love — to be able to love other people; and my search started then.

My mother brought me a present, and when she gave it to me she said, 'Now tell me how much you love me.' Holding her arms wide open, she asked me, 'As much as this?' I said nothing, but after that I became aware that some people give things not for any other reason than to ingratiate themselves with you. I did not answer, I could not answer, I would not answer her. Only by saying 'thank you' did it seem to me that I could get away from this betrayal, for that is what it was.

After my mother's action, I stopped liking her but she was always generous towards me.

First thoughts that I remember about my family are how very silly most of the people who came to visit seemed to be. They represented noise and still more noise. Mother's friends seemed to be dependent upon her, for most of their dresses, hair-styles, shoes and, most important, silk stockings. Once I saw her look of disapproval at one of her friend's shoes — which to my mother seemed to clash with her friend's *toute ensemble*. This one look of fragmental disparagement sent the poor woman home in tears. My mother then went into her rose

16

garden to cut off the dead heads. This fragment of my past, up to then forgotten. A mote of dust caught in the sunlight of her sewing room brings another picture to mind. She loved the deep red of her velvets and of her silks. She had a form, a knack of telling my father when his plans to make yet another fortune would be broken on the rocks of the tough and thieving world. She was always proved right: much to my father's displeasure and to my mother's triumph.

My father was as kind to me as he could allow himself to be. He was, it seemed, always thinking of his past life in Russia. Obsessed with returning, he thought that the new regime would not last. In no way was he practical; in no way could he understand in his bewildered mind the slaughter of his family, being hacked to pieces while he was in the topmost rooms – he was able to witness this work of murder. Some instinct made him run there to the topmost floor, so saving his life. It took my father four months to walk out of his country.

My father and mother were married in 1920. In 1939 he was most kind to me. I remember that for the very first time I sensed he did love me, then he turned away from me. I saw him smile slightly at my mother, then kiss her very gently. He went to his study. My mother seemed unquiet, but she said nothing at all to anyone. She went out into the garden to look at her roses, and weed her own particular rosebed. Then in the silent afternoon I heard a noise out of place. Strangely I sensed that it came from my father. I went upstairs to his room, and saw my father lying face down upon his writing-table.

He was clearly dead. Even then I knew it must have been a heart attack. It was as though his sadness had at last cried out, but too late for love or for help.

I backed away and closed the door. Then I went to tell my great aunt, Gogo's sister, what had happened. I remember that when I told her she suddenly sat down, said nothing for quite a long time, then asked me to say nothing for the moment to anyone else. We went upstairs to my father's room, I following her. She saw for herself that my father was dead, then, turning into the room, knelt to pray, gesturing me to do the same. Some time later other members, sensing that the house had become silent, found their way to us in my father's room.

My mother I think was the last person to get there, and when she saw that my father was dead her distress was terrible to her and awful to every one of us, for we could not in any way comfort her at that time. My mother wanted comforting then. She turned to me; she would always be with me, but I am ashamed to say that I was not able to respond to her needs. The more she asked of me, the less I could help her. Our lives were never destined to travel along the same route. As I felt that I could give them nothing, nor they me, I left.

I left with little money. I had taken bread, a knife, some strawberry jam, and some cheese; underclothes, two shirts, one spare pair of shoes, socks, all of which I put in a canvas bag which I pulled closed and slung over my shoulder. I knew what I wanted to do. It was to become either a singer or a priest. But before this, the most important thing in my existence was the need to love. That is what I was searching for.

Although I was fourteen there was in me the need to regain my brother. It did not matter to me that he had been dead for seven years, the emptiness and the loss was always with me. How can you continue to love someone for that time knowing that he is dead; reliving with him, talking, thinking, making up in my mind and believing that he was still with me, yet knowing that whatever I thought or did, he could never come back from the dead.

Nothing mattered much to me in those mourning years; the relief to be got was in my singing, and the possibility of helping the dying, because by doing this service I seemed to become calmer and to cope in the involvement of dying and helping those who were dying. I was able to assuage my grief. The good death of an adult who dies in simple peace is at one and the same time sad and joyous. Even in coma there is at times some part of the mind that is still able to be comforted. They who are dying sometimes hold your hand, and it would seem that it is they that are trying to comfort you. And at the moment of death I have observed that there comes a tremendous relief and contentment, a gladness that they are over the animal fear of dying, and that death is now what they welcome. For a split second in time, some instinct, some deep inner power, makes you wish to jump that boundary with them, and find joy of peace with them as well. This surpasses all reasonable, all rational understanding, but I have known this to happen to me.

The jumble of my life became an everyday thing. I sang when and where I could. Somehow I remembered England. My father had become for some reason very fond of that country. His business ventures failed one after another, but I remembered that he still had some houses in Birmingham. So I walked through France, getting lifts occasionally. This was at the start of 1940, before the German occupation of my country, which happened on 16 June 1940. I never had any sense of direction. This is still with me now that I am old. The urge to get out of France was the thing that kept me going somehow; nothing other than the need to get away, to step out of that world. I was consumed by sadness and by my terror of madness. My pride, my fear of failing without my brother, forced me to focus my mind into knowing without willing. It is impossible to put it into words any clearer than that, for words to me are signposts to thoughts of infinite complexity, and I have no memory of how I first managed to do this trick of imagining and then realising what I imagined. Perhaps this process came about purely by instinct. It must have done, for in most ways I consider myself to be a dumb ox.

I learned to imagine, then time simply did not exist. So I saw and knew a little of the breath, the force of knowledge, which I absorbed into my mind and body, like loving and losing the best beloved person, which still haunted me as the dark rushing wind of loneliness that kept snatching at me. Then a moment of great elation. I was soaring, my heart lifted in a way I have only known in the loving company of Shura. Shura, I have expelled you, I give you peace. I no longer hope to see you again in my living. Rest in peace, my beloved brother; *libera me, Domine, de morte aeterna, in die illa tremenda quando coeli movendi sunt et terra.*

At fourteen, or just over that age, I became aware of the drabness of the London to which I did not belong; so I did the same thing, which was to look at people. Some kind, liberal people took me into their house, I seem to remember. My English at that time was very limited and very French.

Until I came to England I thought that my love of men was justly right. I knew that many men loved women, and I expected that state of mind to exist, although I knew that I could never love women as much as I could love my fellow men. I understood that most men married and that they had children, but as I never wanted any children of my own I absolved myself of this custom. Judge therefore the astonishment when I learned in hushed tones of voice that to love men in England at that time was unlawful.

I found the British Museum to read in and to spend many of my days there. I was able to sing in the alto voice, and did, but wanted information, as much information as I could possibly obtain. I began by gathering singing teachers by the handful, and became astonished by their fixed minds. As far as I could tell, all of them without exception wanted to put the voice into the mask (forcing it up and into the nasal passages), which was and is total insanity. But I listened to them politely. The English were definitely determined to make a singing sound which was more or a less a hooting, and the more liturgical it sounded the better they seemed to like it. The constant admonition from my teachers was 'No, no, you must put it in the mask, otherwise it sounds uncultivated.' Uncultivated it may have been, but since it was comfortable for me, and as I did have two-and-a-half octaves and had no trouble in communicating emotions and colours to the audience, I thought 'I will have to go on as I am.'

They must have been mad, or mad I must be; someone had to have been right or wrong. Probably they were right; after all, who was I, just by myself, with only my instincts to guide me? But I was comfortable when I sang. I could sing and earn money too. They, on the other hand, earned theirs by teaching, demonstrating with their hands, their lips, their arms; their right arm seeming to try and pull the sound out through the nose and through the mouth as though it were some kind of chewing gum. What 'it' was was never made clear to me at all.

One splendid man intimately connected with Glyndebourne asked me to try and breathe as though I were a telescope. No use at all in my telling him the obvious, that I was not a telescope, and anyway, to the best of my knowledge, telescopes didn't sing.

These, my first times in England, became a nightmare, although slowly I began to understand the English, living in their secret lives and not showing much of their feelings at all to anyone else, and sometimes sadly not even themselves. I started searching for people I could understand and who could understand me.

My alto voice was considered a freak voice. This was long before the days of Alfred Deller, needless to say, but I never sang as a counter-tenor. My singing was full and powerful, and it responded very much like a well-built and smooth-running machine, and it was open.

I think at that age I used my voice in order to find someone to replace my dead brother. I should have known that it was stupid of me to try and replace that love by substituting another one, a new loving perhaps, but I did understand that I was not looking or searching rightly, that I was behaving disgracefully in the true meaning of the word, and slowly I came to know that to love is to give up yourself to the living world. There never is a replacement for the dead, there never is a time when you stop grieving for those whom you have truly loved.

The proposition that there is free will in man is to me unbelievable.

Certain events which have happened throughout my life tell and show with an inevitability that what befell and happened to me, no matter how apart the events seemed to be from those which I thought I should naturally follow, were in retrospect part of a learning path which I have had to follow throughout my life.

That I was older and in another country meant nothing to me. I looked and approached my empty existence without the comfort of my twin, without emotion. London was drab, grey, an enclosed city without, it seemed, any spirit to welcome a stranger. Even its churches seemed oppressed, empty, as though God had turned away from them completely. True that the rituals of Mass were what I was used to hearing in France, but now it meant nothing at all to me, and my first confession was no help. My prayers were empty of any meaning. For the first time I started to sense the stupidity of trying to gain Paradise by observances, both material and spiritual, by lighting tiny candle stars to statues that bore no resemblance whatsoever to the concept of God. I did not lose my trust in Him, but I did start to understand that man had mismanaged, had not understood that God could not grow in the minds of men in any truth by this false theatre, the Church. It seemed that every time I went to Mass it was more and more like a very bad play, stupidly acted and produced. And so, instead of lighting the spirit, it suffocated it with the heavy and deathly perfume of cheap incense. There was no light or love in these churches that I visited.

Then I knew that I must leave London, that sandbagged and bankrupt town, totally preoccupied with itself and without any meaning for me, although this was probably my fault. Whenever I return to London I still have the feeling of emptiness and oppression. I have never slept comfortably there, whether it was the Red Shield Club of the Salvation Army at threepence a night or at Eaton Square – both were uncomfortable, one in the mind, the Red Shield Club most successfully in the body, for it was riddled with lice; and there they turned you out into the street at morning time, after giving you breakfast. The poor of mind have very small chance to survive the compassion of this world.

I remember a young Scotsman of simple goodness and dignity. His path led him to utter defencelessness, and although he was older than I, for some reason he attached himself to me. With him I felt of some purpose, that perhaps I was wanted; and so we became companions. It was now my turn to start telling him the stories, which he listened to as I had done with Shura all those years ago, all those years past. Now I had Tom as well as myself to look after. His company had, in a short space of days, become important to me. His eyes were grey, simple, kind, and the fact that he trusted me utterly gave much joy to my mind and spirit, enabling me to pray once more.

We went to Birmingham, because I knew that my father owned two quite large houses and that his agent had let one of them, subdivided into rather horrible and shoddy flats. The other house was empty, so that I could have it for my own use if I wished to do so. And this I did. With water from the conservatory tank with a pail that we found there, and some rags, we cleaned the kitchen, bathroom and one bedroom. We became tired, and felt as empty as the house itself. Except for old newspapers we had nothing: no gas, no coal, no electricity, no water. We made a form of bed and pillow on the floor from the newspapers, by folding them and sleeping with our coats and clothes to cover us. I remember that Tom smiled and folded his arms around me, and, as if by grace, we both slept. For the first time since my brother's dying I was not alone any longer.

The morning light awakened me. To be aware that someone else needs you is a great beatitude. I heard in my mind, and felt in my heart, love, and the joy of becoming aware that this was another beginning for me. A strange aubade came to my heart when I listened to Tom's breathing quietly, lightly. And then, looking on his simple face and reflecting his total innocence, I was able to find contentment.

In some way my brother came more and more into my mind. But now, with Tom's company, there was much less hurt, and I could remember Shura and tell Tom about my dead brother. And he in his simplicity understood my sorrow. By telling Tom it helped me to become accustomed to the loneliness caused by imprisonment in the human condition. I began to understand why other people were so busily trying to forget that they, that all of us, are always by ourselves, that only loving can alter this emptiness of the soul. I know that loving begins when solitude finds another solitude that protects and is able to touch, to understand and greet the other, even if it be only for a short time; and that if we turn away from this observance we most surely lose our way in this world and fall into void and utter despair, and are quite unable (because of pride, perhaps) to reach out and help others, that we are utterly in a state of disgrace.

Do I hurt people when loving them? Alas, I never will be able to stop loving, no matter however ineffectively I am able to love. How can I tolerate the intolerable by turning away from it, by trying to ignore it? I cannot.

22

I should not have told my mother that I had managed to get to England, but I did it simply to reassure her that I was managing to look after myself and that I was in Birmingham. I did not mention my life, my new life, which I was making for myself with Tom. The way we had met, the contentment we shared between us, was much too important to mention to her, lest she should somehow manage to come between us.

By the end of January or early February we had furnished the house, or rather the rooms that we were using, comfortably and cheaply from second-hand shops: a Victorian sideboard for five shillings, six chairs and a Hepplewhite table for fourteen pounds. A complete Edwardian bedroom suite – a huge wardrobe, a glass-fronted affair with two glass doors, two single beds, a dressing-table, a fine chest of drawers, and matching chairs with cane seats, which I bought at an auction sale for nine pounds, which included some curtains as well. The kitchen furniture again was bought for a matter of five pounds: table, chairs, cutlery, a big pine cupboard which had been painted a dark brown – the stuff of everyday living, in fact, was done within a very short time. Thus I was able to organise our lives. Tom fell automatically into looking after our needs. He applied himself cleaning the house, cooking, shopping, and washing all our linen.

I remember him one night looking sad and angrily at me. Our language, though one of speech, was rather frugal. I think that I must have been trying to communicate with him as I had been able to do with Shura. In my selfishness I had not noticed that my silence made him think I did not need him anymore. He was crying, through my most grievous fault. So I went to him and knelt down beside him. I too was crying, repeating just one word, 'Sorry', again and again to him, until the two of us understood that nothing had changed our need.

He got up and asked me if I would buy him some tools so that he could look after the garden, which had by neglect become completely overgrown and weary of trying to look like a garden. Tom asked me when my birthday was, and when I told him that it was on 19 June he smiled, saying that he would give me a garden on that day. And I knew the feeling of relief, I knew the feeling of joy. Nothing else mattered much at that moment for me.

At night-time we only had the one room where we had managed to black out the windows with some thick rolls of canvas and tar-paper. That room of course was the hub of our living, and the most comfortable to us by far, the kitchen, which had a large cooking range fuelled by coal. The old pine table had been scrubbed clean by Tom so that it had become almost white, resembling the milk which was delivered to us each morning by a milkman who carried the milk in a large pail, complete with lid and ladle, filling two jugs for us, which Tom put on the marble slab that lined the right-hand side of the larder. He always made our breakfast, but the one thing I missed was coffee, because he always made tea which was very strong and dark, and which I never really enjoyed, although I became quite used to it by making it weak. We were not able to get lemons. Tom smiled when I told him that I preferred my tea that way, and that it was strange for me to have milk put in it. I was four months away from becoming fifteen.

I had arranged to have an income of four pounds a week from the house agent who had been looking after my father's property. In those days it was quite enough, more than enough, because by then I had got to know the musical life, what little there was of it. The people seemed strangely easy to talk to, and were in no way condescending. The Birmingham Town Hall had symphony concerts, I remember, on Thursday evenings and Sunday evenings. The conductor was an Englishman called Leslie Heward, whom I got to know and like, and it was he who helped me to get some singing engagements. At first they were not very exciting ones, but it was quite essential for me to develop the habit of performing for small music groups which were dotted all around the Midlands in those days.

My first concert with an orchestra was at Wolverhampton Civic Hall, and I chose to sing the 'Nuits d'Eté' of Berlioz, because it was a work which I loved to sing at that time. I sang as a male alto, and the performance which I gave was very good. It simply came out. The audience had not heard such a voice before, and I still remember the embarrassing response to it when we had finished, because I had to sing it again for them.

The Wolverhampton Civic Hall at that time was quite splendid to sing in. You just floated the sound out; there was no effort at all to work there. It was also the first time that Tom had heard me sing. I think my singing that night was for him, because I knew that I had grown to love him. As soon as possible, I managed to get away from everyone, those people that always come around and must utter platitudinous rubbish to you which has no meaning and always hurt and troubled me, because few of them understood what I was trying to do, trying to communicate. After a recital or concert I had never any other wish than to get away as soon as I possibly could, after I had asked the conductor if it was all right. When we found each other, Tom said that I had done all right but asked why I sounded like a woman. That was the very first time that my faith in my singing wavered, and he never came to any more of my concerts, and we did not speak about my singing anymore.

As the time passed that we spent together, our affection for each other deepened. As the month finished and the new month came to us, I was becoming aware that we were more and more joyous by simply being alone together.

That the country was at war troubled me; young men joining up and leaving their homes was happening then and an important change was taking place in the character of the English themselves. Their reserve, their seeming inability to say anything other to each other than 'How do you do?', 'Good morning', 'Aren't we lucky with the weather for this time of year', continued of course, but as the year passed I observed that they were becoming slightly more communicative with each other.

This was not an overnight transformation, as for example the transformation of Beauty and the Beast:

> When the Beast lies dying he is transformed; the black spell of evil cannot win, it must give way to Death, and Death wipes away all camouflage, and thus Beast becomes Beatitude in spite of his betrayal by the beloved one. And the best beloved one is left crying bitterly, for she has not only betrayed her best friend, the Beast, she has betrayed herself, and by so doing has made herself completely alone.

As an outsider I observed the strength and also the weakness of the extraordinary English stoic attitude. The people were quite unable to free themselves of their reserve toward each other, let alone toward other races, who were branded 'foreigners', some of whom were 'nice' and others who were 'not nice'.

To be plunged by my own wish into this bewildering society was amusing as well as, at times, hurtful. Living with Tom I was learning very quickly that to be accepted into the Englishman's company meant adopting an entirely new character, or I should be politely held very much at arm's length. So I decided to change, to become more accepted into the English system. I had to become another person, as it were.

This transformation thundered on and brought about my next grief, because in my excitement and in my vain delight of shedding, forgetting about my own true self, I managed to lose that which was most important to me – the one person that I had come to love, Tom. One morning he looked at me and called me 'a posh fucking bastard'. He had got his few things together, and without another word he left the house.

At such times, when I am brought face to face with the disfiguring facts of the truth about myself, I cannot speak, nor can I try to alter anything at all which I have caused to happen because of my acts and behaviour patterns. I had lost the person that I had loved the most, through my vanity and my foolishness in trying to become more English than the English themselves; by trying to adopt the bourgeois style of life, which in all honesty I should never have tried to do, because I never belonged, I think, to any specific class. And by aping the middle-class British attitudes, I was disintegrating, I was not myself any longer. When this realisation came upon me, I was ashamed of myself and of my cheapness of behaviour. I had become vain to the point of being intolerable. I was obsessed then with trying to find Tom, but I never did manage to find him. He too had gone away from me forever.

Soon after this had happened, much to my surprise, one morning I opened the door to find that my mother, my sister and my great aunt were standing in front of me. For some reason best known to the fates I was truly back in Hell.

This shocking appearance of what was left of my family momentarily took away my introspection and certainly my solitude. I was faced yet again with a situation that I had in no way anticipated, that I in no way wished for. This appearance of my mother, great aunt and sister was for three years to alter my life very considerably.

They had brought quite a lot of baggage, I remember. My mother asked to be shown where her bedroom was. As there was only the bedroom that I had been sharing with Tom, she naturally said to me, 'Well, this must be my bedroom. You of course must make a bedroom for your sister tomorrow, and for your great aunt.' Which I did, by repeating my journeying into second-hand furniture shops and also remembering that I had to have a bedroom as well. And so the second-hand furniture arrived, complete with rather threadbare carpets. I took good care not to be on the same floor, as the now altered atmosphere of the house became intolerable.

For the sake of my sanity I tried to keep as far away from my mother as I could possibly do, but that was very much easier said than done. My mother was an organiser. My mother knew exactly what she wanted. My mother had to have what she wanted. And so my mother said to me, without flinching and with a complete sincerity that astonished me, that she thought my father had a latent business in Birmingham, and that I had better start it up again so that she would have an income.

I was totally taken by surprise by the sheer force and authority of this request. I told her that I was singing and that I had no intention whatsoever of complying with her demands. She then asked how much this so-called occupation brought in, and when I told her that on a good week I managed to earn twenty pounds, and on a bad week I managed to earn ten – plus the four pounds from the estate agents – she told me that in no way could she manage on that income, as she had to buy food and clothes and material for curtains, and her needs would require much more than my humble income could bear.

So I was faced with the dilemma: should I leave them, as indeed I wanted to, or should I try to combine, to find this business which I had no knowledge of and also manage to sing? For singing was my life, and I had no intention of ever giving that up. After a day of total indecision, I decided that the only possible thing to do was for me to stay, to swallow hard the bile and anger that was swelling and making me angry to the point of utter silence to my people.

For a week I did not speak to my mother, my great aunt or my sister. I went about my empty life as an automaton, completely drained and completely nonplussed by this awful turn of events. My mother became very impatient and asked me what my intentions were. I told her that I would still have to think it over, that I really did not know what to do, and that till I did she would have to wait; for I had become angry, and I was angry still with her at that time in the early months of 1940. I had never expected her to follow me, and I had no intention of running away from a city and from people who had befriended me. Whether they were bourgeois or not, they were all I had.

My mother had no interest whatsoever in my singing and my sister really showed no interest in my work either. My great aunt, on the other hand, was another type of human being, and was perhaps one of the most kind people that I have ever had the privilege of loving. I think I stayed because of her, and because of her great kindness to me as she came to say goodnight one Sunday when I was totally without guidance or any form of energy, when I felt entirely alone and utterly helpless. She seemed to sense that I needed reassurance, for she said to me how much she regretted the trouble that she was causing me. At that moment, and for her, I decided that I would take some action; that I would at least try to run this as yet unknown business venture.

As I no longer had Tom's company or his love, something in my inner mind made me turn to my great aunt to confide in. And when I had told her of my love for Tom, and what had happened to our relationship, she held my hand and told me that she understood, and that to love, that to really have known love, as she thought I had, was the greatest privilege any person could have in this life. She was a most devout Catholic in the good and reasonable sense of that meaning, that faith, that statement.

As I began to observe her behaviour pattern each day, every morning, I discovered that she was already by this time suffering from an open ulcerated wound in her right leg. It was never able to heal itself, and the doctor who attended her could only slightly relieve her pain and discomfort by giving her ointments with which she had to clean the wound, then wash it in salted water, and finally bandage herself again. The wound was not to the bone, but very deep. She never complained once.

She took over the household, cooked, washed, cleaned and loved. She understood my mother and her very volatile temperament, which could alter daily sometimes – in fact she understood, so it seemed, all of our collective doubts and uncertainties. She it was that was able to bring calm to our small ménage, managing to help the three of us tolerate one another. She always laid the table for meals for the three of us, but would never join us. She would sit by herself in the dark and dingy scullery, eating her very simple food. I think that everything that she did each day must have been a form of prayer and devotion, and as such she tried to do whatever it was that was required of her in the day-long drudgery of housework as well as she could possibly do. She ironed, cleaned, and made all the house spotless as an act of loving to us, and even more so, I think, to try to pay homage to the God in which she so firmly believed.

Her hair was long, combed back and wound up into a tight Victorian bun. It was perfectly white. Her eyes were grey, peaceful. She bore a very large mole upon her right temple, and her face was a near-perfect oval, which whenever I looked upon it sang of tranquillity and peacefulness. Her life she had dedicated to looking after her mother and her father, until their deaths, and then had decided to join my grandmother in her task of looking after her family and her household. Although Gogo (my grandmother) and she were sisters, they were complete opposites. It was as though she could not work hard enough or love enough or serve enough in her living days. I think that she was possibly the kindest person that I have known in my life, until I met Michael.

Her hands were neat, and at eventimes she would sit in the kitchen for perhaps half an hour with them folded gently upon her lap. Then she would go the mantelpiece to get her candlestick, light the candle, and silently go to her small bedroom, which was just big enough for her single bed, a small chest of drawers, and a small wardrobe which held her clothes. She wore, apart from the nun's headdress, grey, and could easily have been mistaken for a nun herself.

So the time that we measure in hours and days passed for the four of us.

I think I must explain that my mother was an extraordinary person, although to me she seemed at most times quite impossible to live with. She had that deadly thing, charm, almost amounting to charisma, which could and did attract most people that she came into contact with. She was then in her early forties, still carrying the influence of my father's good manners and somehow a ghost of his Russian background which was totally different from her own. She belonged to the earth much more than my father had ever done.

My mother's father was a farmer, but he also sang, and it was said that he sang well. Although he was a Catholic he married three times, and my mother, Jeanne Blanche, was his last child by his third wife and became therefore the apple of his eye. Perhaps this might explain why in her young adult years, through her beauty and manner, she found out that she possessed this deadly armoury of charm; which once discovered and used such people trade with, I have observed. They soon become the destroyer of part of their persona. The inner peace of mind seems somehow to disintegrate, and there is a great flaw which can never, so it seems to me, be repaired.

Now that I have written this about my mother, it is necessary to say that she did possess an amount of generosity, and that often she could show much kindness towards the people whom she had befriended. Funnily enough, she was able to become the friend of women, as well as being able to charm most men she met. The reason she was able to do this balancing act was simple; she never used her sexuality at all with any of the married couples she met, and so therefore these people, most of whom were in their early forties, were able to welcome my mother without reservation into their circle and into their homes.

At that time my mother could not speak English — I think it must have been in April 1940 — but this in no way daunted her; she simply bypassed the whole problem by going to see the French consul and asking for the names and addresses of all the French people that lived in the Birmingham area. With such simplicity she gained, at the start of her time in Birmingham, a lot of French women as acquaintances. Women who had married Englishmen; others who were half-French with married English connections, and others who were in England for one reason or another. That she attracted people to her was quite apparent. She could become the centre of attraction, although many other women were more beautiful than her. When she smiled she could, without any apparent effort, dominate the small assembly of people who were in the room with her. I suppose she was tall for a woman, but quite plump and quite dumpy, except for her extraordinary hands, which were most beautiful.

My father had given her a very splendid emerald ring which was surrounded by small diamonds. That, and her wedding ring, was all the jewellery she ever wore as ornaments, indeed the only ornaments that she needed. She had not ever worn any form of make-up at all in her life. So her face, perhaps for that reason, or perhaps not, I really don't know, seemed to me to be much younger looking than those of her companions and her contemporaries. My mother's face always seemed an ever-changing kaleidoscope of emotions, so much so, that it was her greatest ornament. That she seemed able to alter her gestures and expressions to suit the person she was listening to or speaking with always amazed me. It seemed to come to her naturally, and although she would sometimes dominate the conversation she could also remain silent when she wished to do so, and in that way at times my mother would become rather beautiful to look upon, although when she thought that she was unobserved the smile would vanish and her eyes would become listless. Jeanne Blanche, my mother, must at heart have been a sad person, probably sadder than I could ever know, probably sadder than my sadness over my own grief. After all, she had lived much longer than I.

She had a habit of collecting new people as though it were a compulsion. This habit seemed to overflow into collecting animals as well — nine cats, two dogs, four goats, many chickens, which always seemed to be running in and out of the quite large garden which had by now become more of a farm-yard than the tidy garden which Tom had made for me, so that by the time I had reached the age of fifteen years there was no sign whatsoever that it had been there at all: it had disappeared, as Tom had done two months before.

For a short time I had not been able to sing very much at all, because by some miracle I had managed to find out how to restart one of my father's business ventures. To my surprise I did this rather easily; again by imagining and then realising the whole. Getting back the people who had worked for my father was quite simple, because I found out from them that they had been fond of him. And so I, his son, had very little trouble in getting about nine of his best people back again to work for me.

In fact, all I did was to make contact with his old customers, telling them that I had found much unsold stock of gold-plated cufflinks which could be simply altered and engraved with almost any forces insignia that would most probably be wanted for the coming year or two, and that I could offer them boxed, padded, regilded, for one-and-sixpence a pair. They jumped at the offer.

My father, the gods be thanked, never did anything in his life by halves, and so we had a great deal of stock, which lasted the small company's requirements for well over two years. The people who worked for me were so good that they did nearly everything — assembling, packing, invoicing, delivering, and even banking for me at the end of each month. They were splendid men, well into their fifties. Thankfully all I had to do at times was to think up new ideas for them to execute; and so the company continued to run rather well and did prosper.

Then I started to sing again, although the mood of war became more and more silent and dangerous. One by one, the streets became blind at night-time and what cars there were at that time had their lights shrouded with what can only be described as looking rather like a tin-topped hat with louvres across it. We were all given gas masks made from black rubber with a form of celluloid window which enabled us to see through, although this window misted up very quickly when we put them on, as we had been asked to do from time to time in order to get used to wearing them if the need ever arose.

Rationing had started. This stunned my mother. Perhaps for the first time the household became much more peaceful, because she was thinking, because she was scheming. Being French, food was a major part of her life; therefore any threat to cut this supply alarmed and galvanised her to supreme lengths and stratagems, in order to have and to continue having as well a stocked larder as she could possibly manage. She was trying to think of an elegant way of achieving this end and dramatically declared to all of us one day, and to the general visible public, that she did not mind facing a firing squad for treason. My mother's views of treason, or for that matter reason, other than her own simple and rather elegant process of thinking, could be at times utterly baffling, sometimes quite charming.

She started plotting and planning how best to overcome this (to her) much more terrifying prospect than the rather nervous fears which most other people were worrying about – namely, German parachutists and bombs. Bombs, she said, could only kill you quickly. And as for German parachutists, she would like to see one try to get the better of her. This must seem amusing, but I certainly would not have liked to be that hypothetical German parachutist landing in our back garden, to be attacked by my mother's goats, let alone by my mother's cunning, or for that matter my mother's rage, which was indeed an awe-inspiring thing to behold. I could well imagine her throwing her precious flour bags at him, and if that failed she would have almost certainly, given half the chance, thrown large handfuls of pepper into his face. This pepper she always carried just in case of such an emergency. Starvation, she added in an awed tone, could take months instead of seconds. It seemed that she was not afraid of death itself, but only the process of dying – which on reflection now seems to be quite right. In the coming weeks she triumphed quite splendidly. By shocking, by bribing, butcher, grocer and baker, she won and continued to obtain the spoils of her particular war. We were very amply supplied with all the food that was available at that time.

Unfortunately she could not keep her dreadful secret to herself, and by tittle-tattling and by telling some of her friends what she had done she found out, probably for the first time, that she was not quite so popular among certain of her more righteous friends, who whether through jealousy or righteous indignation – I am not sure of their motives – declared that she was wicked to do such a dreadful thing. She on the other hand thought their attitude extremely foolish, and could not understand why they did not do the same. Impossible to explain to my dear mother about scruples, because she quite simply did not understand. So she continued to behave and live rather well.

Before I leave these impressions of my mother, there is one rather funny thing which I remember extremely well. Her idea of keeping chickens was well-intentioned, of course, i.e. that we would have a continued supply of eggs. She had thought of everything. She would have all types of breeds that she could possibly buy. She even had two cockerels. Alas, alas, something was wrong with the chicken world. Whether the alarms of the air-raid sirens, which at that time used to accidentally or purposely be switched on just to prepare us for the inevitable bombing, might have upset the biological processes that are necessary for hens of a certain age to produce these much sought after eggs, I do not know, but the egg production from my mother's beloved chickens always proved to be minimal.

Of course some of them, even I could tell, had gone way past the egg-laying stage. She had obtained all her chickens from our milkman, who assured her that most of them after a short time of settling down in their new home would almost certainly give us dozens of eggs a week. This assurance, alas, was in vain, for we never had any eggs, and those eggs that were laid, those few eggs which they managed to produce, were quickly eaten up by the hens themselves. After all, they laid them, I saw no reason why they should not eat them. But my mother seemed quite annoyed, and used to go out into the garden, where she opened the chicken pen door, and spoke very severely in French: 'Now look – if you do not lay eggs for me every day, I will have you killed.' Having thus delivered her ultimatum to these stupid birds, she would stalk off and at times quite resemble them in some ways.

One day the inevitable happened: one of the very old hens died on her. When the morning came she opened the door, and her favourite hen, which she called Josephine, lay inert, very cold, and very dead. After an interval of rather exaggerated lamentation over this dead bird, all was quiet. Then she disappeared into the garden, and we all assumed – that is my great aunt and I – that she had buried the thing. So it was left.

About three weeks after, there emanated from the conservatory a very dreadful smell. We could not for some days trace the cause of this. In despair, my great aunt said to me, 'I pray you, try and find out where that terrible smell comes from.' My mother at the time was out, probably gathering from butcher or baker or candlestick-maker whatever she could get out of them that day.

I went into the conservatory, sniffing, and as the minutes passed by I became aware that the smell was leading me to a very large chest of drawers, which for some reason was in the conservatory. I opened, very gingerly, the first drawer, the second drawer . . . The third drawer proved without any doubt whatsoever to be where this smell of death, decay, putrefaction, whatever you like to imagine, came from. For there the poor remains of my mother's pet hen Josephine lay.

But she was not alone. Indeed, I have never before seen a drawer with a dead hen in the middle of it, so completely filled with very healthy-looking maggots.

I think I took it out at arm's length, staggered to the bottom of the garden, and put it on the general dung-heap which my mother was so fond of telling us was the best sort of manure, if we would only have patience. This, she assured us, would grow the very finest vegetables in about a year's time. I thought that this new contribution would not come amiss – a sort of added bonus. But in my folly I did not realise that maggots quite soon underwent a metamorphosis. And thus we were invaded by a veritable plague of flies for the next few days. The poor carcass of Josephine we covered with some dry leaves.

After a few minutes' consultation with my great aunt, I decided that not telling my mother about her absent-minded form of interment would probably be best, for us at least. My mother, rather like some of our cats, never liked to be laughed at. After a few days, of course, the smell disappeared.

I think at that time my small company was able to give my mother an income of four hundred pounds a month. I had by then decided to manufacture another product which I thought more in keeping with the times of war. I had decided that the company should make hypodermic needles, and talked the whole thing over with my staff, who thought that if the company could purchase certain pieces of machinery – lathes, etc. – to make them, and if the company could get the raw materials, i.e. solid brass rods, and the necessary stainless steel tubes, which of course constituted the entire components with which hypodermic needles are manufactured, there would be no reason to stop us manufacturing them, if I thought there was a market.

So we set up this small plant. The most difficult thing was getting the tip of the needles accurately ground, honed, lapped and polished, with no burr that could tear into the flesh. After this was put right, I found that the demand for these needles grew, and rather soon we had to double our capacity. That little venture turned out to be even more profitable than the cufflinks.

My mother, by this time fired with enthusiasm, suggested to me that I should start manufacturing strawberry jam from beetroot and wood shavings. Knowing full well what was in her mind, I withheld from her and myself the temptation of going into any form of catering venture or manufacturing venture where she could indulge herself in the

34

black market of selling sugar, which I am convinced was at the back of this enthusiasm.

At that time Birmingham was the hub of a thousand trades, and very little changed from the Victorian times of its enormous prosperity, or the even earlier times dating from the Industrial Revolution, when people like Matthew Boulton were making grand brass gas-lit chandeliers and buttons in precious and non-precious metals.

Birmingham was built upon seven hills, as was Rome. There, unfortunately, the similarity ended. Birmingham had its own unholy Trinity at the time of change, the time of revolution. This unholy Trinity consisted of Boulton, Matthew and Watt, who did not in any way resemble the apostles and disciples who were the followers of Christ. They made factories, workshops, and – ugliest of all – row upon row of back-to-back housing for the new workforce, which flooded in from the countryside for money, for work, for a more stable way of life.

Farming in those days might have looked and seemed idyllic, but farmers were quite able to throw out farmhands with their entire families if it suited them to do so. I think everyone who does not work in the country thinks that the country is beautiful: and so it is. The ugliness and the true face of farming, then as now, was well hidden. The large landowners and their land agents and their bailiffs were in some instances benevolent, and gave their workforce decent homes which they kept in good repair; but in most cases the reverse was much more in fashion.

The new homes and the new towns, found very willing slaves to build fortunes for their masters, who built in their turn fine and large and airy mansion houses on the periphery of the lands, the fields, and the farms which they had destroyed in order to set up their ghastly industrial mechanical apparatus. They were the new merchant princes. They raped the land and they raped the people in order to build new money empires for themselves. They thought nothing of making miles and miles of shabby streets out of the once undulating fields and grazing land that surrounded Birmingham in the eighteenth century.

The mean and shabby streets were still there in Birmingham in 1940, and I often found myself walking through those sad roads upon roads of misery where people lived as hopefully as they could. I used to try to imagine what these roads, with these houses firmly embedded upon and into the earth itself, must have been like before this dreadful pillage.

I walked through the Boulton estate, which is on the north side of Birmingham (and at a guess must have amounted to at least three thousand acres of meadow and farmland no more than two hundred years ago), and at the end of this hideous estate was soon on an open road which led to a small town called West Bromwich; along this road I decided to turn right. By this change of direction I found myself looking at countryside and very good woods, paths and hedges.

The sudden transition from the Boulton wastes, no more than half a mile away, took me by surprise — to find free land with cattle grazing in fields so near to the heart of Birmingham. The fields themselves were still quite well-tended. To see a farm house, to read a hand-painted sign with the name 'Hilltop Farm and Riding Stables', to listen to the sound of the wind rushing triumphantly through fine branches, was wonderful.

This had been the home farm of the Dartmouth Estate until coal was found underneath its beautiful countryside. And no sooner than the first two coalfields had been developed and named (I presume with some pomp and ceremony) Sandwell and Hampstead, these splendid people moved away from their rightful mansions and their rightful obligations, sneaking away like vandals to the West Country, or possibly further, to escape their disgusting rape and pillage in the name of making more money, in the name of their utter greed.

I looked at what was left of this once-great parkland, still showing signs of good prospects and a fine sheet of water, still most of an ornamental bridge to cross over and walk upon what must have been beautiful lawns leading you to the now derelict orangery that was being used as pigsties.

And as I took stock of the world as best I could in those days, and what the world could do and had done to a lot of people, I resolved that I must try to continue, that I had to try at least to be myself, whatever that meant. The time of war was now truly upon all of England. What remained of the late thirties and the confidence of that dreadful decade, was fast extinguishing itself; for it was simply an extravagant gesture of vanity and the false values of men.

The time had come, as a surprise to me, that I was now over sixteen years of age. What has already been put down in the past pages continued much in the same way for me, so what use to go into the minutes of my life when I should be only repeating what had settled into an everyday life pattern, an everyday existence? I ask you simply to do a *da capo*.

The waste of days, the waste of trying to help by singing, by finding for my own needs, my own selfish needs, people that I could somehow help – simply to get away from myself, to forget that I was very lonely in my mind.

Wherever I looked, other people receded more and more into their own particular looking-glass. They, I felt, were always reacting to an image of themselves – rather, I suppose, as actors playing character parts of their own choosing again and again. I became sullen, I became infected by the same illness as they, and I was becoming another person yet again.

Soon I felt that I was able to go away from all these empty shallow human beings, but the more this feeling persisted in my mind, the more I became one of these awful people myself. And I started to speak their language, and their language was the simple language of flattery; for the most consuming interest they had was for themselves and their immediate families. The outer world, the world of the have-nots, even in this time of war, mattered very little.

And so I praised them, no matter how much I despised myself for doing so, for I wanted to become acceptable to this society, no matter what price had to be paid.

In order that I too could forget myself, I was willing to become the amusing young Frenchman with such beautiful English. By that time I was able to speak in a most affected English manner. It was very easy; my ear allowed me, in speech at least, to imitate the received and correct English accent. And so, sticking my large Roman nose up, and becoming sickeningly charming and utterly polite, I became rather popular with these totally empty and silly people.

Quite unexpectedly, when I started kissing the Midlands middle-class ladies' hands, I found that this attention flattered them even more, paid to them by a young man who was extremely well-dressed: better, so much better than any tailor's dummy. Rather narrow trouser bottoms, I remember, and good shirts; shirts which were well-made. Oh yes, the right tailors, the right shirtmakers are always to be found whatever, wherever, even in times of war.

Tom had been right about my being a posh fucking bastard. I even started to betray my own nature. I stopped loving. I started flirting with women. This was expected of me for I had come from France, and some of these foolish people thought that French men were perhaps somewhat more romantic.

This state of affairs went on for some time. I was still managing to sing. The voice was very much firmer than ever it was in my younger years, its power surprising even to myself, the range was still the same, yet inside myself I felt a great distaste for the noise, because it was beautiful and I was not. It sounded a very strange noise to come out of a young man's body, and I started to become ashamed of it. Yet another proof of my not being able to know myself.

Perhaps most of the good elements of my dual being died with my twin brother. I had lost the balance of his goodness, which I knew he possessed, and for that reason I felt in disgrace.

It took many months for me to stop hating myself, to clean my head and heart of my wrong self, and to know and to understand that I was shipwrecked for the rest of my life in an unwanted, an unwished-for infinitely weak body and mind and heart, and that I could do nothing about it but continue to piece together what fragments, what good there was to be found inside my own vain and poor mind and my mean spirit.

What was I running away from? The answer was simple: I was running away from fear, because I did not want to be hurt any more and because I was a coward. Not able, not thinking, but willing, and, worst of all, no longer loving because of my wilfulness and my vainness of spirit.

I was taken by extreme despair of heart and mind; and then began a deep purgatory because the best gift, the only worthwhile thing which mattered to me, had vanished, because I was no longer able to wish to love.

I had lost my trust in my faith through my last confession. I spoke of my being able to love men, and the damnable person who heard my confession – I could never think of him as a priest – condemned me for what, to me at least, was and is still the most precious thing in my life. He was so utterly wrong to wound, to break a human being thus. Where was the compassion, where was the love, and how was it possible that the Church had misunderstood so gravely Christ's teaching and Christ's loving? How had His parables, how had His sermons, how had His behaviour become so distorted and disfigured by this complete inability to understand what loving meant, what loving is, and what loving is meant to be?

The only consolation I had was the goodness and wisdom of my great aunt when I bitterly recounted to her my anger and my despair and helplessness. I also told her that I would never be able to attend Mass again. Not only had I betrayed myself through my utter foolishness and vanity, but I felt betrayed by my Church just as much.

I was stranded in a world and a country at war. I was also stranded in my own personal war that I was losing against myself, and because of myself. I was angry and I was afraid.

At this time my mother had made of our house an hotel for the Free French Army and Air Force. This annoyed me because sometimes I had to share my bedroom with a total stranger. At times there would be as many as six young men spending their leave with us. My mother simply put another bed in my room, never bothering, never asking if I minded or not. Up until that time my bedroom had been my only escape: my music and my books, my piano; my table and chair by the window. I was able, by looking out of my bedroom window, to see park and meadowland which belonged to the Leverett estate.

These young men that my mother made welcome were in most part good and were very pleased to be in a French-speaking household, but without exception they were interested in *le dancing*, *le sport*, *le sex* and of course *le food*.

To be surrounded by all these simple young men for one reason or another enabled me to regain my balance again, making it quite understandable to me that it was not possible to go along the same route as they were on. Let them take the world, let them take their narrow pleasures; I did not want the same world, I did not want the same values at all, so therefore in hindsight I must thank them for showing me quite clearly that that path, at least for me, had to be rejected.

My mother was in her element. My great aunt was more and more loaded with work, in fact worn out by this time, for she it was that had to do all the housework as well as all the cooking – that is until I lost all control of myself and told my mother that unless she find quickly, very quickly, help for my great aunt, I would not give her any money. I do not think she had until then thought that any of her actions were in any way less than admirable ones. She did not even understand that I, with my staff, was supporting her and her particular needs. The thought that she was dependent on other people – myself being one of those people, but more particularly my staff – had simply not entered her mind. As she came to realise that my anger over the matter was real, and that she had been using my great aunt almost like a slave, she suddenly became sad, and perhaps for the first time I saw my mother in another light, a kinder one. I saw that she was shocked by my accusations. I saw that she also came to understand that my great aunt was already an old woman, and in much pain.

About this time I began to notice that my great aunt was always touching very lightly the walls of the house. One day the soup tasted extremely bad. I did not bother to finish drinking it. Looking up, I was amazed to find that everyone else, including my mother, was grimly finishing the damn stuff. Indeed one man was looking rather sick, and it was unfortunately the night that my mother was entertaining her hero, the great man of France, de Gaulle.

My mother was much sought after by the Free French administration, because by that time she had opened quite a lot of so-called charity shops for the Free French and contributed rather large sums of money to that organisation – most of which went into quite personal forms of funding, I was to find out later. The officers loved her for her contributions, and therefore they had arranged for the great man's coming to dinner. My mother was transported, of course.

I have no recollection whatsoever of talking with him that night. I just went as quickly as I could possibly do so to the kitchen, and I was just in time to observe that the cheese which had been used for the soup was Sunlight soap. Then and only then I understood that my great aunt had become quite blind. The rest of the meal was cooked perfectly, after all she had been cooking and slaving for us for years.

When the weekend had passed I spoke to her, asking if I could help her in any way. She asked me straight away how long I had known of her blindness. When I told her that it was only over the weekend, she seemed relieved. I did not mention anything about the soap, and I told my mother never to mention that particular sad matter to her. Even in her blindness she had never complained to any one of us. This great distress she kept entirely to herself. Unbelievable it might seem, but it was part of her saint-like quality simply to bear just yet another burden, simply to acknowledge that this was part of her destiny, simply to understand that this was best for her. And when I looked into those now blind eyes, I suddenly knew that I loved her very much. I think that my mother also felt ashamed.

The turn of the year 1942 has started.

Imagine a young man – you have read about him – and his family, and some of the events which have happened to them. Think if you can, if you will, about the times that he has written about, and what is going to befall him now.

Should he continue, should he go on with this shadow play which is really just the start of his life? What will befall him in the near future; should he continue in the first person; should he write in the third person; or should he try to write part of it as a play? This is an experiment; so let it begin.

The scene is a house in Birmingham at the start of 1942:

Jeanne Blanche	The young man's mother
Tante Blanche	His great aunt
The young man Shura	Aged sixteen years
René Ramond	A French Air Force gunner who is on his first leave with them. His age is twenty-five years.

Sitting-room. Curtains are drawn. René Ramond is sitting in the small armchair near the fireplace. He is dressed in his dark blue and gold uniform, which is made from serge. His face is not large and he has fair hair which is cut very short. With him in the room, talking to him, is Jeanne Blanche. Her hair is a rich brown chestnut colour which is slightly greying at the temples. She wears it tied up in a chignon. Her dress is very simple: it has a lace blouse which clings rather closely to her neck.

She goes to the door after pouring him some wine, asking him to excuse her for a time while she finds her son. She then goes out and closes the door, leaving the new visitor alone. He looks round the room and waits, and he is wondering if this is going to be just another of those ghastly visits with some awful people yet again. Her son enters the room. He too is very bored, because he has done this welcoming ceremony many times before and he has a preconceived idea that this meeting will simply be a formal one of welcome, nothing more than that.

He walks in, and very suddenly stops dead, becoming quite rigid, and is unable to say anything at all. He is just staring at this man, who is by now smiling at him.

Somehow the most difficult thing for Shura to do is to close the door, because he senses that if he does do so his world will never be the same again, because for the first time since his brother's death he has been able to communicate with another person without speaking.

René seems also to recognise that there has been a meeting, and a very unusual one for him. He gets up from his chair and walks over to his younger host, just looking at him.

Shura is thinking that he knows that he is able, badly this time but nevertheless to some extent able, to communicate with another person again without speaking. Only this time there is a stumbling, and also a great fear of death, of dying again. But he also knows that he is not alone any longer, that he has at last found, however faint, the resonance of one mind being able to communicate with another who is able to respond to him well enough to make him know comfort, find an end to the sad silence of his mind which he has lived for all the years since Shura's dying. The greeting from a total stranger as yet unspoken to brings a strength which until now he thought would never reach him again.

And so a love began between these two strangers. The younger man shaken, the older man also shaken in just the same way, just as surprised. They both understood that fate caused this meeting to happen, yet both realised that it was the most wanted thing for the two of them.

René spoke to Shura: 'Well, my friend.' Shura could only cry out, 'Help me, please; I have been lost!' and René answered simply by saying, 'No longer.'

The very best gift in the world had been given to these two people. The gift that the earth and the gods could bestow upon man, the gift of loving in the perfect silence, in the peaceful depths of the mind. That surprising joy of knowing that they were as brothers, able to love one another.

René thought, and Shura was able to understand his thinking quite clearly in his mind, and what his mind received was simply, 'Shura, I am with you.' But by then he had lost all control of his mind. Shura became like a brainless creature; he completely and utterly failed to carry out the mathematical operation of continuing this wonder. He decided to cut out the silent dialogue with René; he would only use words this time. The other way was too much to have to bear again.

René seemed to understand Shura's plight, and he spoke out to him, saying, 'As you wish, until you are no longer afraid.' Then they tried to make sounds of speech. Speaking formally, Shura pointed out an early Victorian bookcase which he had just purchased, saying that it was rather a find, and that he liked it. René smiled tolerantly, and continued with the game, for he knew that Shura did not at that moment trust his emotions, that he felt vulnerable to the point of near rejection, and René did not wish this to happen. Their relationship was one which he had never thought could happen to him, and his first bewildering thought was, how could he tell Shura that he was married? – as was the case. He sensed that Shura would not be able to understand this, because he

42

had never been in love with a woman himself. René was quite incapable of deceiving this young man, of that he was certain, but he loved Shura with an utterly different love that he had never expected to find. Shura was looking at him and René knew that Shura was going to tell him that he loved him, and that, he knew, was what he wanted to hear him say.

At that moment Shura was nearly crying. He remembered pulling the door open, not knowing that by his action in doing just this simple thing he would be in turmoil, disturbed by his meeting, and knowing well that he was in love with this stranger he had just met, because he had recognised that this was yet again another sign that his life was preordained, that there was no choice in the matter.

As a rule, when he was at home at this hour, after greeting and meeting yet another person, he would, as soon as he possibly could, excuse himself by telling the visitor that he would have to leave him, because he had some work which must be finished. Now the thought of leaving René alone with his mother and sister did not enter his mind. So, when they both of them came in, he remained with them, falling into the normal conversations, the normal observances, which he no longer cared for.

His sister, he felt, did not like him very much. This did not matter to him. He could never bring himself to dislike her at all; it was simply that they had very little to share, very little to say to each other, a lack of common interest. His mother of course held the stage – which she could always do if she wished. That night she started to praise her daughter's good qualities: how very well she played the piano, and how clever she was, and how good she was at dressmaking. Shura's sister could not sew at all, could not sew a button on any better than her brother could. Nevertheless Jeanne Blanche continued in this vein, saying that her son Shura had of course some qualities as well, but she just knew that he, our new visitor, René, would much rather be left alone with her daughter. Her son, anyway, she felt quite sure had something that he wished to do before dinner. Shura's mother was always trying to marry her daughter off to someone she felt to be desirable and suitable. A certain quality was needed, she felt, a certain accent and a certain breeding, and René was quite obviously the most suitable material that she had encountered thus far. She always had good taste when it came to finding possible young persons of marriageable age for her daughter.

René looked up and said that he would of course enjoy her daughter's company, but he serenely asked her if perhaps he could help Shura in any way. This surprised Jeanne Blanche, and she murmured something or other, at a loss for a reply, because she had not expected this reaction from him.

René turned to Shura's sister, asking if she had any pressing thing to do other than entertain a perfect stranger. René was most definitely able to convey without any difficulty whatsoever that he preferred her son to remain with him. Then he dropped the small bombshell by asking Jeanne Blanche and her daughter if they would like to see a picture of his wife. This had the reaction that he had wished for, because both mother and daughter suddenly decided that it was perhaps a little later than they thought, and that they had better help with the dinner. So after another five minutes' chit-chat had passed, they got up as gracefully as they could and left the sitting-room.

René went to Shura, sitting near by his side, and told him that he loved him, and that if it was possible he wished to be with him as much as he could. The younger man had known that his rapport with René was absolute and he could only grin and say 'Of course', and that he had two concerts that week – one in Dudley and the other in Leicester. He asked René if he would like to come with him, saying that he would be very pleased if he did. René replied that as long as they could be together, whatever Shura had to do was perfectly acceptable to him. He asked Shura what he played, and when the reply came telling him that his friend sang, René asked him if he was any good. 'Without a doubt,' came the reply from this now content young man.

At dinner Jeanne Blanche was charming to René. She told him that her son rarely made friends with any of her French guests. René answered that he could understand very well, that he too found it extremely difficult to make friends in his life; there had to be fondness and there had to be interest, and then he added very simply that of course, love was not to be found easily for anyone in this life, thus telling her in his truthful way that he had formed an attachment with her son. She merely smiled, and told him that she was glad; she also told him that her son was much too engaged in running their factory and therefore she thought he would be very busy most of the coming week.

René asked her how her son managed to be a professional singer as well as managing a business. Jeanne Blanche told him that it had not occurred to her that there was any difficulty or any conflict about that. She added that she knew very well her son had to work hard in order to sing, although to her so much effort for little monetary return

44

seemed unwise. René told her that he supposed her son did not simply do it for the money, and that perhaps he did it because, as an artist, he had to express himself by singing, and probably the singing was more important to her son than running a business.

By this time Shura's mother was becoming rather annoyed with René; no-one before had become interested in her son's singing. He asked her if she went to hear him perform. She said she did not like a young man to sing in that manner at all and that it did not seem natural to her that a young man should have the voice of a woman; she simply could not understand how her son, she continued, could manage to sing like that in public at all. She sniffed, and then remained silent.

Then René looked at her, and turning to Shura asked him if he would show him to his bedroom. Jeanne Blanche replied rather spitefully by saying that, as we seemed to get on so well, perhaps it would be nice if he and her son shared bedrooms. René smiled, saying that he would be delighted to do so, and asked Shura if he minded sharing his bedroom with him. Shura had already decided that he would welcome René absolutely. He knew that he could not hide any longer from this man, that he would welcome him entirely with his whole being and mind, because he understood that René had already reached out and found his hiding-place of grief.

As they went upstairs, René carrying his one suitcase, they were quiet. When they reached Shura's bedroom, Shura closed the door and turned on the electric light switch, revealing the room.

René, observing it, turned to Shura and said, 'The icon is beautiful. Do you have faith still?' His young host replied that he did, but as he was homosexual the Church damned him; that he felt bitter over the crass stupidity of such thinking, and until the Church changed its mind he could not go to Mass again.

From the silence of silence, of total imprisonment in himself, away from the world which had become a museum of sadness until this meeting, this moment, this new loving with René. René, who he had not known for very long, René who had freed him, René who had made him for the first time since his brother's death able to sound, however feebly, to contact however feebly another human being's mind.

René on his part was earthshaken. He had a week's leave with this strange young man. He had never really thought that he could feel this love for another man; yet he had somehow welded an indissoluble bond between himself and Shura. René asked about Shura's life, and when Shura told him about his life until their meeting, René became amazed, and said that he found it very difficult to believe. He asked Shura again and again if all these happenings in his life had occurred, had been true. When Shura replied yes, they had, he laughed incredulously and said, *'Mon Dieu, mon Dieu, quel vie, quel complication et quel misère!'*

Misery it was, complications I had never thought of. Complications that I had to work through. I then said to René, 'But it is nothing. I had to do these things because there was simply nothing else to do.'

And so the whole night passed in talking, and as the morning came, they were still not tired. René said, 'What's the next move?' Shura looked at the clock and saw that it was six, and said, 'Well, my great aunt gets up at six; let's go down and have breakfast.' So they went down; and they had breakfast with his great aunt, and the bowls of black coffee, and the bread, this time English, and the yellow butter reminded Shura of his brother, and of the time that they spent together in Blankenburg with his grandmother Gogo. Suddenly René said to Shura, 'Why are you looking so distantly?' Shura answered very simply, 'I am thinking of my brother. I am thinking of the time that I spent in the late summer with him and with my grandmother, who said it wasn't natural for us to be able to converse silently.'

I could only explain it badly in words, but the communication that I had with my twin was a silent soundless language of the mind, and I had a tiny resonance of that from René. But of course it wasn't the same. René said that he too felt a probing, a message without words that was coming from me to him.

My great aunt smiled. As I have already said, she was blind, but she heard from our voices where we were; and she went to René, saying very, very quietly, *'Vous savez, monsieur Ramond, que mon grand-neveux est très innocent* – you know, Mr Ramond, that my great-nephew is innocent when he speaks of love. It is not a particularly carnal thing.' René of course seemed to understand this, and assured her on this matter. And our week together began.

It began by our simply being together. He accompanied me in what was a boring round. He went with me to Dudley, where I sang. After the concert was over, he came to me and said, *'Mon Dieu, mon Dieu, quel voix, que c'est fantastique! Je n'ai jamais écouté une voix si passionée. Ce n'est pas une voix de femme, c'est une voix, n'est-ce pas, insupportablement triste* – It's not the voice simply of a woman, it is the voice of unsupportable sadness. Now I believe your story. Now I understand you. Now I am much closer to you.'

And Shura knew most positively that he did understand, and for the first time the reassurance that was so needed, and is needed by all artists, had come to him at the right moment. After the concert they were walking around the very dark city. They had a total absorption in communicating with each other.

This jumping about from first to third and then back again is the best I can do. If I use the third person, it seems less painful; I can distance myself away from the events that went before.

In 1942 I met René. In 1943 I would have to declare myself as a pacifist. I naturally spoke of my pacific views to my great friend and companion, and although he could not understand, he did respect the simplicity of my outlook, which was basically that violence bred violence, that war bred war, that killing was murder.

I was so terribly afraid that I would lose René. I think right from the beginning we both of us knew that this was likely to happen. He said that if he should die, I was probably going to find other loves, that one love led to another. I replied to this, 'Yes, yes, and I know this, but I do not know if I can bear the suffering of losing you. I don't think that I can.' He then reversed the tables and said, 'Well, supposing you should die; I don't think I could bear that. I think that you probably have more courage than I, and I think that you would somehow survive, as you survived your brother's dying, because although you call yourself a coward, you seem to have managed to survive. So let us live from day to day, from leave to leave. Let us try and absorb as much of each other as we can; let us be together when we are permitted to be together.'

And so the first week of loving finished; and as Shura accompanied René to the train, he was openly crying. René, although not crying, was visibly upset. After the train departed, Shura felt lost. He managed somehow to go about his work. He had René's address, and immediately wrote to him. After a day, René's letter came to Shura. Shura's letter came to René.

René was going to be moved to York, and he said in his letter that if Shura could possibly manage to come on Friday he would have a weekend leave, as he was not flying that weekend. And so, knowing absolutely that it was more important than anything to see as much of René as possible, Shura wrote back saying yes, he would be there.

The meeting was an extraordinary reaffirmation of the love between the two of them. There was a strange hiatus. René had to be back in camp by eleven, and there was no doubt that he didn't want to leave Shura, as Shura didn't want him to go. René had managed to smuggle one of his friend's uniforms out, and his pass. The only resemblance between his friend Emil Soulace and Shura was that they both had large noses. René said, 'Look, you change into this, and I can easily get you through, so we can at least talk through the night.'

The camp was vast, and quite frankly nobody knew anybody else, especially as the Free French contingents were fairly isolated. So for the first time, in a hotel cloakroom, he helped Shura to dress up in a Free French Air Force uniform. And when it was done, this change came upon Shura, who had never expected to wear any military uniform at all in his life; and when he looked in the mirror as he adjusted his peaked cap, René smiled and said, *'Mon Dieu, mon dieu, que vous êtes très bien comme un jeune officier. Voilà, quel transformation!'* Shura blushed.

There was no trouble getting into the camp. His room was deserted; his three colleagues were on leave, and so they were left to themselves, talking continually till morning came. At that age they did not understand or know the meaning of becoming tired.

As they walked through the streets of York, they came across most improbable names. They came to a name which completely perplexed Shura, because the street was called Whipmawapmagate. Shura sensed in York a great and terrible presence of history. He told this to René, who answered by saying that he also sensed some terrible foreboding – whether the foreboding, he said, was for them or something that had happened in the past history of the town.

He asked Shura how his interview had gone with the authorities and Shura answered that, as far as he could tell, it had gone as expected. He had expected that these middle-aged men with a total sense of purpose, with fixed and preconceived ideas of what was right and wrong, would have no respect for him as a pacifist. They put the usual questions to him about what would he do if he saw his mother or sister raped. He said that he would try and do all he could to stop it. They just nodded their heads, and scribbled the word that Shura still remembers, which was 'coward'. He restated that he would not fight, that he would do nothing.

René asked Shura what he was going to do, and when he was told that they were going to send him down a coalmine, René said, 'My God, my God, you of all people down a coal-mine! I can't believe it.' Shura assured him that it was quite true, asking 'Why ever not? It seems cleaner than killing people.' René answered that he supposed it was, given Shura's philosophy on war.

I think that the year was very difficult for me, as companionship

48

and love for René grew and developed. At that moment in time there was no doubt in my mind that I wanted to be with René for the rest of his life, for the rest of mine.

I must stress here that René was far more sexually attracted to women, and that this caused some friction between the two of us. When I tackled him about this particular aspect of our relationship, he answered, 'You must take me as I am, or not at all. You have to accept that side of me as well, which until I met you was totally dominating my interest.' After some time the only practical thing for me to do, of course, was to accept that this was part of the René that I loved; that this I could never change. It hurt, but he pointed out that I in no way wanted any physical contact with him, and I said that that was true – all I ever wanted to do was to lie close by his side and talk, and discuss, which we did very often.

The idea of love-making was totally abhorrent to me. He respected this, and I came to respect therefore that he had to have his *soulagement* – his relief, and that when we used to go to *le dansing* he used to sort of wink at me and whisper that he would be back in half an hour, which always was so, perhaps five minutes, perhaps ten minutes more than the half-hour.

And so I used to wait for him, and after the slaking-off of his sexuality and the obvious relief that it brought him, our companionship and felicity continued. So I soon became used to the fact of his needs, the fact that his sexuality was in no way a threat to our loving. I think that Shura loved René as much as René loved Shura.

The total complication of 1943 was enormous. René intensely disliked the idea of Shura becoming a miner because of the dangers. Shura's dislike for René's fighting or René's killing or the probability of René being killed in his gun-turret was equally great.

The time came for Shura to go down the coal-mine, and the experience became an everyday thing, which was a total surprise to him. It was also a total preoccupation, for this was an entire world that he had never perceived, that he had never imagined – this training and the abominable conditions underground. Paradoxically the friends that he made were a sort of counterpoint to his anguish at being unable to be with René all the time. He quickly worked out the most sensible thing to do as a so-called coal-miner, which was to work the night shift. This was not a productive shift; it was a maintenance shift, putting things right that the two day shifts had in their working hours inadvertently dishevelled, causing machinery to malfunction.

And so it was that Shura became an electrician's mate. A very lowly job, the lowest of the low in fact. This was an extraordinary time in his life. It took three experienced coal-miners to look after this idiot who could not even work an endless motor. The endless motor consisted of a continuous spiral of wire rope. It was perhaps one of the simplest jobs to do in the coal-mine, but even this he got wrong, because he could not understand the code of signals. When they wanted him to stop, he carried on. This was not only stupid but dangerous to the men, who decided to make him, as it were, their mascot.

The initiation rites were rather unexpected and horrible to him. His reaction to having a ferret put into his trouser pocket was not one of enjoyment. Mercifully he stood still, and thankfully, after an age, the bully whose Christian name was Bert took his damned ferret away again.

They eventually let him tuck himself away in a motor-house which was not in use, with his books, where he could cause them the least possible havoc, the least possible damage. They could breathe a sigh of relief that that bugger – Bill, they called him – couldn't bring death and destruction on all of them. They had the charming habit of creeping up on him when he was asleep; they thought nothing of pissing in his water-bottle, or putting a dead mouse in one of his sandwiches.

The discovery of the polluted water was for nine or ten seconds unbelievable to his senses. But when his senses told him what he was drinking, and slowly the word 'urine' came to his mind, he vomited – much to the delight of his onlooking companions. When he came to bite a mouse's head off in his sandwich, there was another round of nausea and of utter revulsion from Shura, who did not know how to behave under these peculiar practical jokes – for that is all they were in fact, to use a peculiar English colloquialism, 'to knock some of the corners off him'. I do not think corners were ever knocked off, but after six months of this very extraordinary teasing, he was able to correct the imbalance between these truly splendid men and his truly ridiculous naivety. He could not blame them: he was a constant source of amusement to them, and they were after all kind enough to put up with his complete inexperience of their world, and of their somewhat rustic ways.

Shura thought that the coal-miner's life was very hard; he formed a very high opinion of these extraordinarily courageous men. Once he was very frightened when part of the mineworking tunnel collapsed, cutting his party off from their colleagues. The collapse was caused by

50

what was known as a 'bump'. He was lucky enough to be with some senior miners who had been in 'bumps' before, so that when he lost his head and was very afraid that they would be entombed by this fall and would die a rather slow and horrible death, they just told him not to be such a fucking fool, and that it would only take about thirty-six hours for their mates to dig them out. They were quite marvellous to him, for they comforted him. They were indeed a breed apart; basically gentle folk, doing perhaps what was one of the most terrible and dangerous jobs that our world could throw at any human being. And after the initiation ceremonies, which seemed de rigeur, they befriended him, and on more than one occasion saved his life.

In the meantime, however, as much as he could, he continued seeing René; continued also to give as many recitals as possible.

Towards the end of 1943 he decided to audition for a repertory company, and as he was in Birmingham the simple thing to do was to audition for Sir Barry Jackson, who was head of the Birmingham Repertory Theatre in Station Street. He wrote asking if Sir Barry would be polite enough to grant him an audition, where he would sing them two arias, one in Russian and one in French. The first aria would be Boris's 'I have achieved the highest power', which he sang in Russian. The second was from Gounod's *Queen of Sheba*, aptly titled 'Lend me your aid'. By this time Shura knew exactly what to do on the concert platform as a singer; and thus he became an actor student at the Birmingham Rep., the lowest of the low again – Assistant Stage Manager – which he continually got wrong.

Now he was expected to learn part after part every week. Some of the members of the Birmingham Repertory Company were very kind and good to him, because without any doubt he was the worst actor that any of them could ever remember seeing on stage. When Sir Barry Jackson asked him, 'For God's sake, Shura, why do you want to be an actor?' Shura told him that he had no intention of becoming an actor, but that as a singer it was absolutely necessary for him to understand what stagecraft was about. Sir Barry Jackson was very tall, very kind. Time and time again, Shura would make mistakes on stage. Sir Barry's retort was a sort of resigned, 'Typical, typical; for God's sake do try not to kill anybody, including yourself if possible.'

On the occasions that Shura was on stage, the wonderful cast, the proper actors, used to come and see what this total idiot, this buffoon would do. . . . Out of the door and say as M. Poirot, 'Ah, good evening. I am so sorry to disturb you. Pray forgive this intrusion.' This he did, word-perfect. It was unfortunate that he entered the drawing room through the huge fireplace. It was also unfortunate that as he was leaving the stage he got hold of the door and pulled it instead of pushing it, thus bringing down quite a large chunk of the scenery. The audience thought it extremely funny; the cast thought otherwise. But, as I have said, they were very kind.

As for Shura's Boyatt in *Loves Labour's Lost*, his speeches were delivered dramatically. He was quite appalled when somebody hissed in his ear that this was a character part and that he was supposed to be funny in it. That piece of information made Shura freeze, made him forget his words, and so he did the only thing that he could possibly do, which was to fall down and somehow mumble on. Unfortunately the king and his companions were not amused, and no amount of leaning on a sycamore tree could rescue this Boyatt from being absolutely abysmal in the part. All his follies and all his stupidities on the stage amounted to total absurdity. I do not know to this day why they put up with him as they did.

Shura at this time was very well-occupied. He was learning German with a rather large pear-shaped German who had the splendid name of Gottlieb Rotenburg, who was endlessly writing very bad philosophical tracts, which it seemed to Shura would be much better read to a psychiatrist. An example that Shura remembers very well from his dear Gottlieb Rotenburg was as follows: 'I like to sit, I like to lie, I like to feel the grass between my fingers. I think of my beautiful mistress and her carnation groin' – etc., etc. But never mind, Shura somehow got through this jungle of German sentimentality. One morning Gottleib opened the door, and pronounced, '*Ich bin einen sentimentalen Traumer*' and Shura could only answer, '*Ja.*'

The actual severance from the great Birmingham Repertory Company came when Shura said, yes, he would sing in *1066 and All That*. But when he was given the music he nearly died with horror at the sheer unintelligibility, the sheer nonsense of this dreadful work. No way was he going to sing 'We are going home, we are going home, on the road that leads to Rome'.

Shura's subsequent refusal to act was going too far; he was called to Barry Jackson's office, which was on the second floor, and was told that it would be a very long time before he, Sir Barry Jackson, would give Shura further work. And so it was that Shura's acting career was, just in time, nipped in the bud, for I am sure that Shura would have

52

made a stunning actor – or perhaps more a clown than an actor. And thus passed most of the year 1943.

The year that René Ramond, on his last mission, was killed. Shura heard of his death almost immediately. René had requested that Shura be notified immediately of his death. He had said that Shura was the only relative. He lied to the authorities, in order that Shura would be the first to know.

That small oblong envelope, the telegram, told Shura that his relative René Ramond had unfortunately been killed on his last mission, that they would be sending on to him what few effects René Ramond had, and that they would be burying him in Harrogate military cemetery at 11.45 in the morning on the coming Thursday, if Shura wished to attend the interment.

News that caused Shura to become yet again numb, angry and alone. He decided that he would go the day before René was to be buried. He had not been to Harrogate before. When he eventually found the right place, the undertaker's place of business, he was allowed to see his friend René: all he could do was weep.

The loss in the corridors of his life continued. It seemed to Shura at that moment in his life that he had been robbed and pillaged. He was not able to understand the reason why he should suffer yet again the bereavements which seemed to dog him.

René's wife, when she was able to, came to find his grave. She asked Shura to tell her of their friendship. Shura answered her by speaking as simply as he could of their times together and at last he found the courage through sheer necessity to tell her that he, Shura, had loved René.

Her sadness seemed to enable her to understand. She told Shura that it was her wish to have René's earthly remains returned to his native soil. Would he, she asked him, help her by being at his graveside when the disinterment happened, and would he, Shura, identify her husband, René, for her? She was not able to bring herself to do it, she told him. So Shura said that he would. The thought of his task frightened him very much, lest he could not bear to see René dead: René whom he had simply loved.

The identification took place. He could not stop himself from vomiting. The stench of death came to him as the coffin lid was removed. In death René's face had shrunk, and there was an unshaved look. As Shura saw his dearest friend, he felt the never-ending river of torment, of pain, flood him, drown him. He kissed René his last goodbye, and after that he managed, in a very cracked voice, to tell the authorities that this body had been René Ramond.

René's wife had asked Shura to bring her back a lock of his hair, but in his state of distress he had forgotten to give her anything other than an account of the disinterment, and that indeed she would have her dead husband to bury in their family vault. He tried as best he could to help her until she had to return to France.

Before she left, Shura gave her a small parcel which was all that remained of his beloved friend René, all his earthly possessions. He had destroyed their letters. The letters which he, Shura, had written to René meant nothing to him, meant nothing when he consigned them to flames. They did not hurt him. Burning René's letters did hurt him, however. He only wished at that time for René himself; nothing which reminded him, nothing, no shadow or photographs, could make up for René's absence. Shura only wished to remember René when they had last met, when René had told him that he only had one more mission to fly before he was grounded; and for once Shura had not been so worried, knowing that it was his last mission. He had convinced himself that it was going to be all right after all. He had no idea that their last meeting was their goodbye, that it would be the end of their loving; only the essence of their great friendship would remain in the shell of Shura's mind and heart, because the pathway to René was now closed for ever.

> I did not see the world the day you died,
> What is life when we have finished it?
> Only a blood begotten machine
> That for a time we live in.
>
> We on that first day felt passionate intensity
> Lurch then fly for us.
> King of my past living
> I can only whimper your epilogue.
>
> We used our bodies with innocence
> and found a terrible love.
> Love now is dead for us you and me,
> The day you died, the day you said goodbye to me.

Although René was dead, although Shura became silent and found it impossible to sing, the silent dryness of his life had to continue, with routines which had become his life pattern. He wrote to his agent asking him to cancel all engagements, because he knew then that he would have to change his voice and by so doing try to become another facet of his mind. He even thought of changing his name and try to become quite English by this method. But he gave this game up very quickly. He had to continue as Shura nothing, but still what little he had must not be altered, only circumstance, only experience should mould him. He was alone but this was not new. His great aunt comforted him. Overnight Shura stopped singing in the alto voice – by turning it around he found that he could sing an octave as a very light baritone – although the way of singing as an alto was totally different and without effort. The new sound on the other hand was another matter. It was breathy and he could not control it at all well – it was also unable to respond to his mind or to his thinking. So the long path had begun for him yet again. He had to learn a new method. He had to find a teacher to help him in order to do this transformation. This was easier said than done. The first teacher in his new voice was himself. He had by this time read much on the subject of singing – finding straight away that all differed in fundamental facts. All without exception avoid the most important information – which was of course comfort. All of them spoke of the voice as though it did not belong to the body – as a separate thing. This of course was utterly foolish. One book written by a Mr Ernest White was entitled *Sinus Tone Production* implying that the tone must be kept there and going past the stage of madness by saying that even if the larynx were removed the act of singing would not be hampered! This nonsense and more ill-informed teaching made Shura research as well as he could by himself. By going back to his old voice he gradually found out what he had been doing all of his singing life, namely that his alto was open in the middle of his range, that the so-called top was most certainly moving by itself into the head cavities, that the back of the throat seemed, when he was singing top notes, to become larger. That the larynx, the higher the voice went, moved completely down or much lower in the throat. That the reverse happened when he sang lower tones – it, the larynx, moved up. Then he began to think of his breathing – in alto the voice and the breath behaved as one, that they were in some way connected. But in baritone they were most surely not, in point of fact that they were acting against each other. In spite of these troubles after some months he was able to try out his new voice, he was able to sing his two octaves somehow. For him the lower part of his voice was very much more difficult to make stable. The top, if he covered it in a certain way, was easy and not nasal. That it did not need very much cover at all, a form, a sensation of beaming as it were from the larynx to the back wall of the throat, as far back as possible as though he was starting to yawn. So from that place where he was yawning the beam of sound moved of its own accord, when it wished to do so, moved into the head cavities, for some form of reflection of sound, then came back, to come out from the mouth. As he became aware of these sensations the voice became more stable and some of the old comfort in singing returned, although he still found it impossible to co-ordinate the breath with the voice well enough. What he had naturally in the alto voice was not in his control as a baritone. Although the voice grew, although he started getting work as a singer, he knew that it was impossible without a method. The teachers he studied with always wanted him to sing – when he asked about the start of the tone they simply smiled saying, 'Don't worry, it's all there.' Shura knew that they were not able to understand the importance of breath and launch of tone – that they themselves were not able to do it, that they spoke rubbish. That they did not understand that the body cannot sing unless the breath is always supporting the tone, that the thin column of air has to be always in the right place under the larynx in order to support the sound. Willing makes a prison of voice. Thinking with the inner mind frees it.

Paris, when Shura went there towards the end of 1945, was most beautiful. Although the war had just ended and there was still very much bitterness between the French who had collaborated with the occupying German forces and those who had not done so, although the bitterness of that dichotomy was still in the air and was still tangible to some extent, this did not stop the city from being beautiful.

Shura was unable to disenchant himself from walking endlessly along its streets for the first few days of his reaching that city, smelling strangely of the country, of garlic, cigarettes and that extraordinary tang which is quite unique to Paris – of very good cooking, somehow uniting with those enormous sewers.

The River Seine was also much more approachable along its banks, where he was able to walk, where he could almost understand its grey calmness. For him all rivers spoke differently. The Seine was a reassurance to him in a way.

Shura felt at home in Paris. He had met a few persons who interested him. One man in particular was, like himself, a writer.

The simple fact that they liked each other was surprising, because the only thing they shared in common was the fact that both of them wrote poetry, which they read to one another. Alain thought that Shura's poems were much too complex in form, and in no way sufficiently clear and down-to-earth. Shura thought that his friend's work was rather too agricultural, and written in a form of metre which he did not find pleasing. Surprisingly though, they did seem to get on well with one another. Alain the extrovert, Alain the bold conqueror of the world, Alain the ex-Resistance fighter who still had a few pounds of matière plastiquant with which he used to blow up railway tramlines and whatever else that he could to hinder the disagreeable Germans.

One night, because they had nothing better to do in the deuxieme arrondissement, they decided to blow up a pissoir. After making quite sure that no one was in sight, not even a cat or dog, they did this very percussive thing. There was nothing left of the Clochemerle utility. The lights went on and the high middle-class French and very respectable people that lived in this wealthy central part of Paris opened their shutters, shouting, 'My God, my God! The Germans have come back!'

Looking back, Alain and Shura were quite awed by the deed, by the anarchy that they had brought about. The only trouble was that there was no reasonable excuse for them to have caused this diversion, this mischief, which strangely, mystifiably thrilled Shura. Alain was seized with further ambitions of demolition, but Shura told him that one explosion was all the excitement that he wished to be involved in.

There were a few people that he wanted to know. When he was in Birmingham he had met Ninon Vallin, the French soprano. She had just sung for the Free French cause. Shura's mother was always arranging that sort of thing. After the concert, because Shura had admired her work, he went to meet her, telling her that he had much enjoyed her singing, and especially her Schubert. She seemed very surprised by his picking out in particular the Schubert songs that she had sung. She asked him why, and what he particularly liked about the German songs. Shura answered her by saying, 'Because you sing them in a manner which is forthright and exciting to me.' She asked him if he sang, and when he said he did, she asked him to sing for her.

When Shura had finished singing a Fauré song to her, much to his surprise he found that she had been crying. She told him to go on singing like that forever. She had not heard a male alto voice before, and she thought it was splendid, and asked who had taught him to sing like that. Shura replied simply by saying, 'No one.' He just sang, and had done so since he was very young. Again the question was put to him, where did he get such an intensity of feeling from? He answered that he was not aware of it, that he was more interested in striking and binding the notes, that all he wished to do was to express what the song meant to him.

The concept of language, of image, linked to music, and that in turn welded to the intuition which drove his mind and body to express some part of it, at least to try to do so, was the only thing that he as a singer could possibly hope for.

One day he telephoned Ninon Vallin, telling her that he was in Paris and could he come to visit her? She replied, 'Of course. Please come to see me tomorrow morning at 11am.' Shura thanked her.

The next morning he gave Ninon Vallin a small bunch of violets as he paid his visit to her, for which she thanked him. She asked him to sing the Fauré song again that she had heard him do in Birmingham. But when he started to sing for her, she screamed, very musically, and told him to stop. Where, she asked him, had the voice that she heard gone to, and what was this baritone voice doing or trying to do, replacing his extraordinary alto voice, which she had found uniquely beautiful?

Shura was very distressed by her reaction. He told her that whatever she thought, he would never be able to use the high voice again. She told him to sit down, that they had better talk. In the end Shura told her his reason for no longer wishing to use the alto; so much had happened to him, and he always associated his alto voice with the things that had been unbearable. He told her, 'I want to forget, if at all possible, my past. I want to make a fresh start, hence I have to try and make a different noise to help me. Please understand this. What is the use of bothering you with my past life and my past pain, of my past remembrances that I must try to forget, for you see I've written it down simply to expel the hurts that haunt me?' Ninon Vallin replied by saying, 'My dear, we all have suffered in our lives, and I doubt very much that throwing away what you could do so well can help you at all. But as you appear to have made up your mind to do so, I had better try to help you as best I can. Although I do think that you would be very much better working with my friend Reynaldo Hahn, so sit down please and I will telephone him.'

This she did; and Shura met Hahn two days later at Ninon Vallin's home. When Reynaldo Hahn walked in, Shura was surprised. He was short, slim, sprightly. Reynaldo Hahn on his part seemed taken very much aback. He asked Shura if he was a writer. Shura said that it was very difficult for him to divorce his writing from his singing, and Reynaldo Hahn said, 'How curious. How intriguing. You remind me very much of a very dear and close friend I knew long ago. But as I am here to hear you sing, I had better do this.' So on this midday Reynaldo Hahn sat at the piano and proceeded to sing himself. Shura was totally enchanted and totally captivated by this extraordinary man's musicality, and by the sheer capable knowledge and conviction with which he was able to sing. Here was a master singer, here was an intelligence, here was someone he felt totally at home with and intuitively felt would be able to help him with his singing, with his method. He felt a calmness and an assurance.

I envy those chroniclers who assert with reckless and sincere abandon, 'I was there, and I saw it happen. It happened thus.' Now I too, in every sense, was there, yet I cannot trust myself to identify with any accuracy the varied events of my own life, no matter how vividly they may seem to survive in recollection. We are all, I think, betrayed by those eyes of memory which are mutable and particular as the ones with which we regard the material world – the vision altering, as it so often does, from our youth to far age. And that I have by devious and unexpected routes arrived at old age is a source of some wonder to me. I could say that I know all things which are recognisable to me from my own experience, but what is the use? Because whenever I look at the map of recollection it seems to be an ever-changing thing.

All the ghosts which haunt are dead now. Their memories have vanished away into the stillness of time, which has had its nights and its days of torment. Seen through present eyes, times long past fail not to hurt. The ship that was taking me back could at any moment vanish, as vanish those that I have loved, vanish they most surely have. But I would somehow conjure them back again if it was possible. And surely it was possible. Ghosts really never die; they are simply abandoned. People make new ghosts for themselves when the old ones become bitter as bile vomit.

After the death of Reynaldo, I wanted something which had belonged to him. I walked along the streets without paying attention and without direction. It was winter time, cold and bitter. The year was 1947. I did not frequent my friends, and I had no wish to sing. I became entwined in a nightmare of grief; I was not able to cry out, 'Not fair, not fair!' Reynaldo's death takes me back again to my brother. That we were freaks, my brother and I, is a truth that I somehow manage to disguise, to hide from myself, although I think I always knew from very early in my infancy. I wonder what would have happened to our relationship if he had not died. That shattering relationship had to be held up, remembered, and yet put aside for someone new, with whom I could take up and perhaps complete my living and the dialogue of living, which, rising out of the ashes like the Phoenix bird again and again, reminds me that I cannot leave Reynaldo. I cannot forget anything which belongs to the past either, which passes ever more into the present time, resulting in a blend which is super-real.

One morning I called unexpectedly early to visit Reynaldo. Before seeing him I went to the kitchen, because I wanted some very hot coffee to drink. There was a young person that I did not recognise, who I had not seen before. His smile seemed to me rather nasty and sly, and I did not wish to be long with him, so I took the coffee into the studio where Reynaldo was playing Fauré and singing, as well.

He stopped when he saw me, telling me that I was a welcome friend. Then he said, 'It's time to listen to you now. Do the Opus 113; I shall play for you.' Which he did. When we had finished, he asked me to learn Fauré's last songs, a group of four called 'L'Horizon Chimerique'.

Another thing I remember is his asking, 'Where did you learn all that intensity which comes out of you as you sing?' I answered that I simply did not know, and realised that I had no wish to speak of my inner thoughts, that my wish to sing had grown from the loss of the people who were beloved to me – the first being Shura, then Vassily, then René, because in those days I never spoke of any one of them. Soon I should be without Reynaldo.

He began to tell me of his own life and his own problems. He spoke very simply of his life, which I think must remain in my head and not be written about. I shall simply tell you that I was beginning to grow to love this man who was so much older than me. He took my arm and looked for a very long time into my eyes, then kissed me quite simply upon my brow.

The maid came into the room, telling him that he had a visitor. He lifted his finger to his mouth just once; turning to me he said, 'Let's try to get away through the other door', which led us through the back part of the house into the garden, past the dripping rain-soaked trees, passing everything and everyone as we got to the pavement. And he just said, 'You are my last great adventure. Do you know that?' He left me then, asking me to visit him that coming night.

The avenues, the streets with their klaxon noises, the bistros with

60

their yellow-gold light, and the strange perfumes of Paris, of Gaulloise cigarettes, garlic and drains, and on top the smell of small cafés with their fritures and their escargots and their steaks with Pernod of aniseed smell, which drowned my head. I was young then. Reynaldo was old. He had taught me by example, and if he wanted to lie close to me then so be it.

This is my story, such as it is, that bitter year full of present time. And time is a constant reminder that past, present and future are undividable, always carrying us into ourselves, and perhaps sometimes others as well, whom we meet.

The shop windows reflected the unknown members of the world, and as I looked I saw young men and women walking, mostly blankly unaware of themselves; and amidst the unknown crowds, grown suddenly black in the dance of night, I took out my matchbox to scrape a light. There in the plate glass mirror were images of the ones that have mattered, and those whom I have loved. The catafalque of life which I saw then held me away from despair, turning my memories into invisibilities of loving, travelling companions who would always stay with me.

My loss was very great. I can only retreat into the past, so making my future Shura alive again to me. I have to slow down his reappearance. A bridge has shattered time. I am looking at the rose window, the great rose window of Nôtre Dame in that dusty church with its pennants in tatters. It has a nimbus of time, a large time of truth encircling its beauty. Shura is younger, and he is no longer cold in his future grave. Not here, not now. At last we are face to face again, and I ask, 'What are you doing in these parts, Shura?' His eyes are laughing.

I picked flowers and gave them to him. He outstretched his arms to welcome me and said, 'I am still earthbound in you, because our time together is not yet finished. How will it ever be until you set me free?' How can I stop remembering him? We were walking along the path which took us to our streams which we had partly dammed with stones and lumps of grass-rooted earth pulled up from the bank side in order to make a tiny pool which we seemed never to tire of looking into, how in the matter of a few short days plants were starting to appear as had small beetles and other water creatures. We also looked at each other, finding many truths, invisible to non-twins. Were we 'monsters'? The name comes from the latin *monstrare*. A being that is 'demonstrated', put on show, and were we not ever to escape that fate.

The dark wave of tomorrow that never comes, the wave of memory that quickly escapes becoming tangible. Shura felt that the hurt in his life thus far could only be expelled by the act of singing. This meant the total abandonment of what was considered to be the so called conventional way of singing. When he spoke of this to Reynaldo the latter smiled and told Shura that in order to do just that, he, Shura would have to know, to understand method. Before he could break the rules, he would have to understand them as much as possible. He would help him, although his voice was limited in power, and therefore he could never exceed any distance of intensity. By this time Shura's voice was becoming stronger again. This strength seemed to excite Reynaldo Hahn. He was Shura's first mentor, the first to understand that Shura's need for singing went far beyond making beautiful sounds, that Shura was searching for the meaning of the poem, that there had to be two lines: one music, one words. That just to sing melodically was simply not enough, that the words' meaning had to implant themselves into the voice.

So they met Reynaldo Hahn and Shura. Reynaldo was intrigued by this young man, this slightly built person with dark brown hair, dark brown eyes and a rather large roman nose, who had the disconcerting habit of looking directly into his eyes. The voice was good but his method was non-existent, should he try to teach him, would he be able to start absorbing what he had to teach him he wondered? At least his speaking voice was well placed in the larynx and that he supposed was as good a start as he could hope for from this young man.

Reynaldo's way of teaching was exciting yet baffling to Shura because Reynaldo was always singing himself for Shura to listen to. Shura could only be amazed by what Reynaldo Hahn could do, and when he asked how he got a particular sound Reynaldo simply replied that he got it and that was that.

Slowly Shura began to understand that although interpretation and method were both necessary, the versatility and the ability to act and sing came from a very solid method. Reynaldo Hahn would talk about the absolute need for support of sound and the correct way of breathing, dismissing altogether the diaphragm, and telling Shura that he must breathe much lower and thus neutralising the crippling power of the diaphragm. The lower the breathing the more comfortable the voice became, and there was always support. But at that time the sound was supported more by luck than by knowledge of what to do in order to co-ordinate the breath support with the stream of sound.

One day he asked Shura to sing him Lully's 'Bois Epais'. When

62

Shura started to sing this aria he suddenly felt the despair of the words and music, when he came to *'je me plus pas suffrir le jour'* he broke down his eyes wet with the sorrow of the loss of all the people he had loved in the first two decades of his life.

Reynaldo stopped playing, saying nothing at all but looking directly at Shura. Then he asked Shura to express his sadness – all of it – to him. And so started the process of understanding, perhaps for the first time in his life, his past loving, the greatest of which was the loss of his twin brother which still hurt and grieved him, now more than ever, it seemed. It was as though the Lully aria released the closed door of remembrances that finally Shura had to confide in another person.

Reynaldo held Shura's hands and wept with him saying he understood, telling him that he must express all sorrow which he had imprisoned within himself. Shura could only cry out that he could not and was not able to continue being hurt anymore, that gross fear held him.

Reynaldo told him that grief and suffering had to be borne by every human being, that he too had by now lost the few people whom he had loved. He told Shura that when he was young he had loved very dearly someone very like Shura, that it seemed possible to understand grief because he, Reynaldo, had been able to love, that sometimes death was better, kinder, than was the usual human condition of watching the beloved person lose interest in him.

He told Shura how he, although afraid, had fought in the First World War, that others had thought him brave, but he did not think that at all. He simply tried to get through hour by horrible hour. He still remembered those young men's faces as they died, as they suffered, some dying without arms or legs, torn and broken from shells. He leant over to comfort Shura telling him that simply to live was a joy.

> This strange museum
> This gallery of the past.
> This travelling, this mind
> This death, this fear!
> This love, is all there is,
> All that could be asked for.

Shura was starting to feel comfortable, was starting to enjoy being with Reynaldo as much as was possible. One day he noticed that Reynaldo was not well – and within seven months Reynaldo was dead and Shura was alone. The year was 1947.

Shura watched the days of winter after Reynaldo's death and wondered what he should do. If there was any knowledge that he had acquired in his life up to that time to be of use, it was simply to go on, and not wait for events to find him. He must find his own tomorrow – more than a singing teacher was needed.

Pierre Bernac was in no way able to fire Shura. In fact, they rather disliked one another. Bernac thought that Shura was impossible with all his questions. All his rejecting of his dictums which seemed to Shura thoroughly shallow and vain – sad also that such a man of noble intelligence should settle for so much second-rate and out-of-date whimsy in his own work. All the dots and notes were observed. But no damned voice and very little interest after the first half hour – in other words tricks of past success which should not be repeated for simple repetition of so-called success – a success by the way which was never much thought of in France. At that time only the English thought anything much of him in the late forties. True he had good diction and he was very tall, to Shura at least. He quacked his way through most of his singing. He sang grammatically well, but he never really seemed to be a true singer. For some reason the relationship continued. Bernac damning everything that Shura did. Shura knew what he wanted to express and tried to do that, but time and again found that what he wanted to do with his voice was just too insincere and that the poem could not be served enough. His method would not let him do anything other than sing loudly or softly very nicely. He wanted more – much more. Bernac could not understand this, although he paid lip service to the needs of interpretation. To Shura the great divide was always there – music first, then rather like an echo the words would form themselves but somehow not belong to the event the music was trying to evoke. For him it was becoming impossible to listen to other singers who sounded simply beautiful, who seemed content to go through the motions and intone their way – sometimes dreadfully and liturgically boringly.

After Reynaldo's death Shura drifted. The first thing was to try and remember his dead mentor. Again the burning of letters seemed necessary for Shura to do. So this he did walking one morning in the countryside just outside Paris where he and his older friend walked and spoke out random words. It seemed to Shura that Reynaldo would welcome the action of discarding the emerald and gold ring which had been given by Reynaldo at the beginning of their friendship. Shura took it from his finger and threw it out to the calm dark water. Then he burned all the letters which Reynaldo had written to him. By the water's edge where they had been destroyed, he picked up the fragments of charred paper and placed them upon the slowly moving waters. Then, after many hours, he returned to Paris.

I am sitting alone in a shabby restaurant. The striking blank faces around the tables eating and drinking. Talking became a murmur, a sea upon which my mind glided over fishing out words from random speech which filled the room. A flood of talking, talking which wrapped me up in itself, making new pictures for me. Sometimes there is a woman's plaintive voice breaking through the chorus of absent-minded everyday conversation, becoming the Prima Donna of this shabby opera for a moment, only to stop, to become drowned again by the sea of murmuring which as nightfall approaches seems to focus and become sinister and disquiet fills the place. There are more people now and as I am alone at my table I sense that someone is standing by me. I look up and become aware of a young man. He is tall, and gives me a cigarette, which I take gratefully. I thank him, I look up into his eyes, and notice that he has fair cropped hair, which is perhaps cut a little too short; the brow is high, and the smile is a simple uncomplicated one. His hands are lean and well-formed. The clothes which he is wearing are looked after carefully. He says, 'My name is Jean-Paul,' and sitting down beside me says yet another thing: 'I have not seen you here before ever. Why are you here in this sad place? You look quite lost, if I may say so.' Then he asks me who I am, and what it is I do in life.

My simple reply was that I had walked out, walked away from my teacher that I had begun to love, and that I had no wish to see him laid out in yet another coffin. The ever-sweet smell of death which is common, or was common in those days to us all, was more than I could cope with, as I had seen enough of it. I told him that I had not the slightest wish to do anything, or even to think very much; time was passing, and already the night was old. He said, 'I would like you to come and stay with me for a time.'

He got up, and he held out his hand to me, which I took. The night was black. We walked along the streets with their ugly shattered shops and houses, some of which as we passed beside them were letting shafts of light filter through their shuttered eyes and making grey-silver rays fall into the street's black pools which lined up forever in that district which I had gone into in my despair. Its shabbiness comforted me. The fact that I was with a complete stranger, walking along with him hand in hand, comforted me too. Jean-Paul was, I suppose, more trusting in me. I felt that I had trust of myself; the silence and the noise of the night-time made our silence to each other right, simply proper. Until we reached his door we did not speak.

His apartment, which he had painted throughout in light blue-grey, had long narrow doors and windows, which were painted a dull Chinese red. He turned around as if seeing it for the first time; then he said to me, 'You are welcome.' So it was then that I looked into his face and observed his calm. The light of his eyes touched me with pleasure, and for a moment I saw Vassily standing in front of me again. The remembrance of Vassily whom I had loved so much after Shura died returned and shook me, like a thousand fears that shout and growl into our deepest rivers of fear, of pain.

Then the time returned to the present night; I came back from the past. I was looking at another person, Jean-Paul, who said, 'You always look solemn, as though sadness fills your face, and you have no mask of joy to hold before you. I wonder if you smile; I wonder if you can smile. And by the way, I should like to know you by your name. So please tell it me.' So we formally introduced ourselves to each other. Then he said, 'If you had not told me your name, I would have had to invent one for you. How can I love you otherwise?'

His voice is filling me with memories, and I am no longer in the present. I am aware that Shura is close to me again, and soon we shall be together. The stairway which leads me to him is of the earth and of the sky, and in a burst of light he is with me.

There is inexpressible love for him, he is not dead, he is a grown man. That was the genius of my creation, and so in that present land where past lives here and future time comes and goes like passing breezes, like everlasting timeslips of the mind in this garden of remembered things, events grow like a fever in me. So as in delirium the beasts of fear which govern all of us clamour to conquer, making it impossible not to perish or drown in the gutter of man's futile attempts at living. But beware though, and remember that the bitter taste of fear shall be forgotten as quickly as vanished pain is. Remember this.

I said my farewells to my friends; France held so little for me, the last person that I wanted to say goodbye to was Jean-Paul. That young man and I had shared more than a passing time to-gether. He had shown me kindness. He had shown me encouragement and love. It was he, now looking back, that had been my tender

66

friend and lover. In those few last weeks together we appeased and satisfied each other's lusts, and I am not ashamed to write this. As we bid goodbye to one another, I think that it became clear to Jean-Paul that he was not the long ago person that I was still longing for and knowing that I should meet and share my living with, and could not meet in France. England called me back for that.

I shall stop writing about my other singing teachers – until I met Joy McArden I was in a void, not only because there were none whom I could work under; my third decade was a mess. In retrospect, between the ages of twenty to twenty-eight undoubtedly were bad years for me. I suppose it was then that I started to behave rather childishly. In those years I became quite selfish and unbearable to myself, let alone my friends. True I was getting more engagements and the noise seemed to be liked. But I think through lack of method I was limited to sounding more like a musical instrument with not much colour. The audience wanted sustained top notes and top notes they got, got very loudly if I remember.

In the past when I was very young there was no reason why I should not be at all truthful in my writing of these worlds – I always realised that I was going to be the outsider in this my life. It seems that as I grow older that I am learning, that I am just beginning to understand the thin voice.

I do not want to write at the moment. I suppose I never do, the start is the horror of doing so, always. Picking up memories of the past which has brought me to this pleasant country. Which is for me the most beautiful time of my life. I go back to the old rooms of my past, the people whom I knew and worked with and the things which I managed to do.

Something within me forced me to do, to have to do, many things all at once, to sing, to find the singers who moved me, the teachers who made me grow, to help me and guide me. Joy McArden, an unfamous Wagner singer who gave me for the first time the comfortable open sound throughout the compass of the voice. The first position and how to launch the vowels without distortion. The other great goodness was the fact that she never asked me for money, the fact that for the first months she insisted that I must have the first lesson of the day at nine o'clock in the morning, the second at 12pm and the last at 4 pm and as much as possible. That we managed to carry this through without murdering each other was surprising to the both of us. The pure hell of trying to launch 'Ah' to her satisfaction and my despair was amusing. Ah is Ah, sounds simple but to strike and bind I found sometimes a near impossibility. The more I tried the worse it seemed to become, all she would say was 'No, again please.'

No singing, no songs and I only wanted to sing. But No! No! Not until I was able to launch the sound that she alone knew was vital. The first time that the 'Ah' noise came out of me she smiled, closed the piano lid and said 'Let's go out and have some coffee and do not sing at all for a few days. Simply try to remember the noise you made. But don't try to do it by yourself.' On reflection it proved to be so simply done because I continued to remember the sound which seemed to come from below the voice box and much more from the trachea which seemed to work in together with the larynx and become one part.

My great aunt died in 1953 aged ninety-four. Many years before she had written me a letter to try to console me. As a post scriptum, I suppose it belongs to the last page of this work.

> *Mon Cher Shura*
>
> I know that you have suffered much when your brother Shura died, I know that you have been grieving and searching for him, never forgetting him, all this I know. I understand that you have grieved also when the few others whom you loved also were taken away from you by God's will. There is I am sure a fate which we cannot escape. Throughout my life I have done the only thing possible to help you, and to thank you for looking after me and caring for me. I have prayed that you should not become bitter or resentful but most of all I have prayed that you will find love and so learn to love God who is above all things.
>
> May you always keep your faith; that at the end of your life you will turn to him.
>
> With all my heart I wish that.
>
> God bless you and keep you for the work he has chosen for you to accomplish.
>
> Your loving,
>
> *Tante Blanche*

68

This is then the prelude of my life. To write of singing is impossible, to sing is only what matters in these recollections no matter how badly done. Are the shades the ghosts of people that have made and helped me towards the ever moving objective, sound structure, shape the words and notes meeting in the mind? There can be no fixity. There cannot be any easy route to what foolish persons call style. There is only the mixture of music and poetry, which comes to life in the mind's remembered experience of the life interior and exterior and most important of all the instinct of knowledge far beyond your remembered times. The whole of my living has driven me through pathways which have all been sign-posted, pushing me sometimes obscurely into the night-time of sure understanding. That I am not compassionate enough to encompass the acts of loving which I have encountered in my life. That I have failed to love enough; that I have not understood enough or given enough, that I can never be enough.

7 January 1994 Sherri Gehman.

Shmuel Guterman 1978.

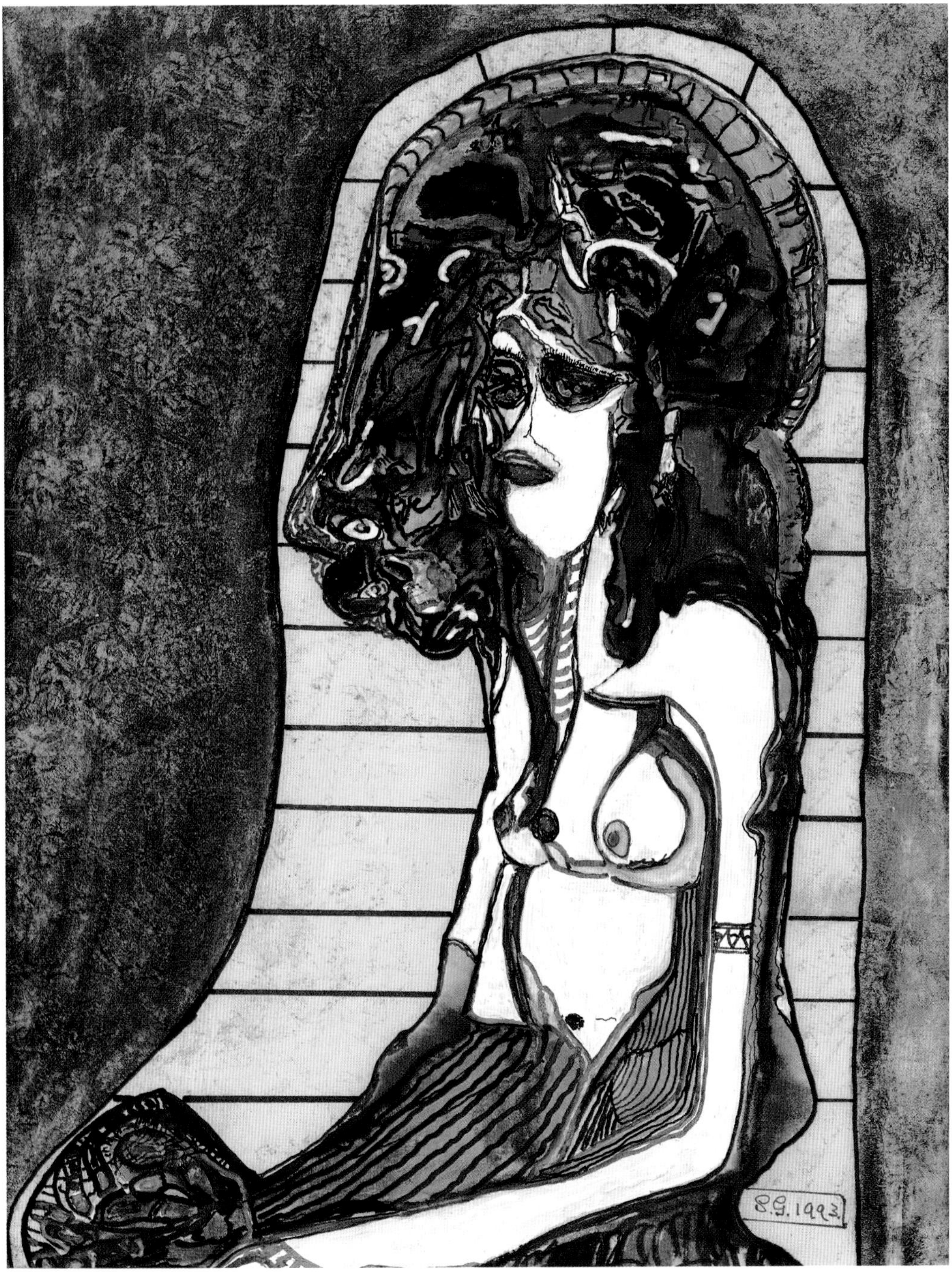
S.G. 1993.

2nd November 1.35 AM.   Shuvo Rehman 99.

14

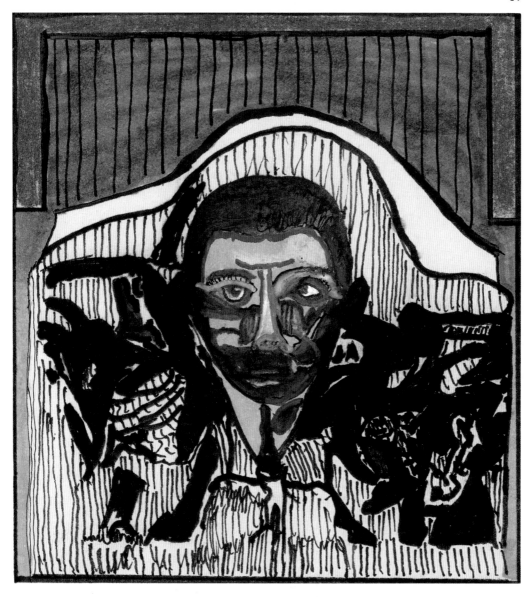

21

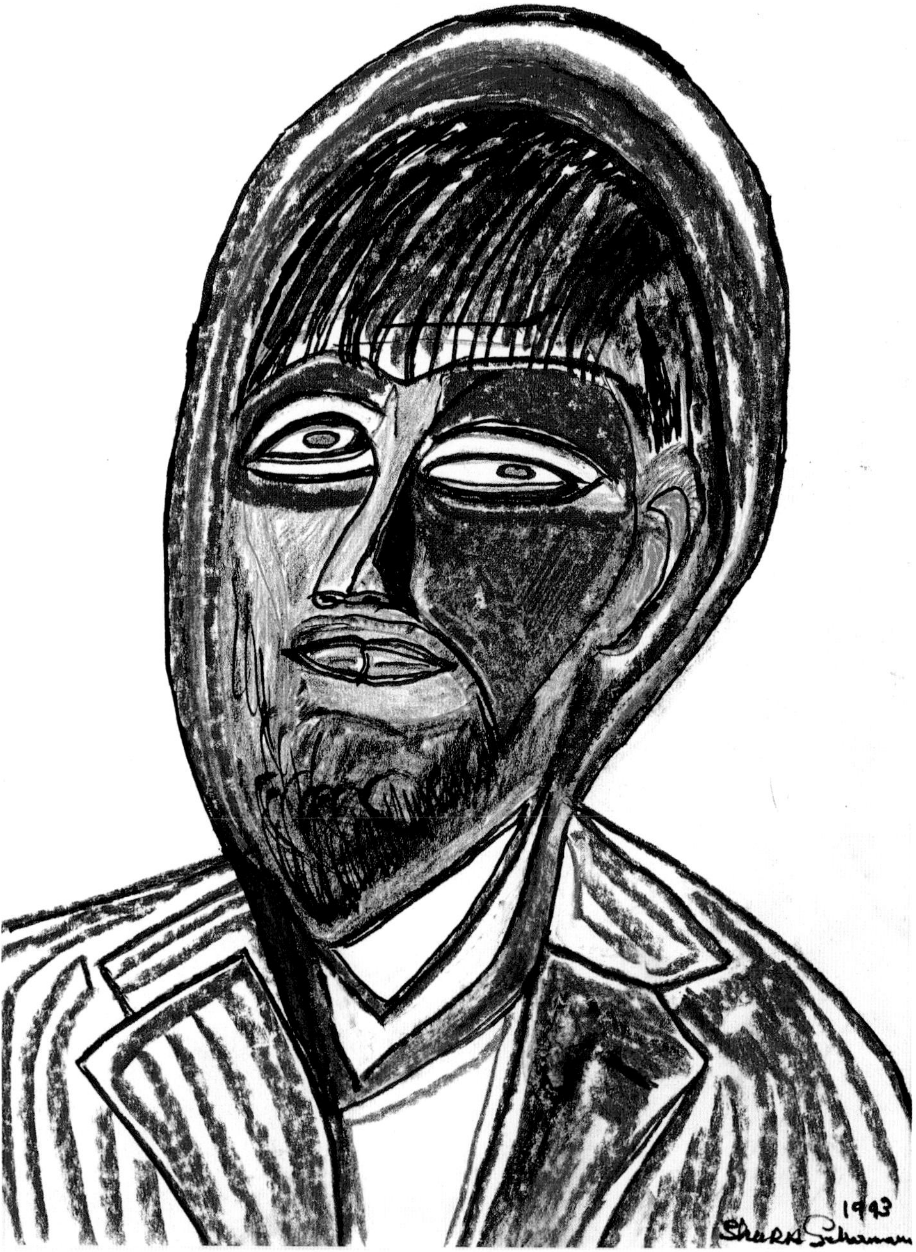

4th November 8.15 am finished.   Shirin Gebremen 1998

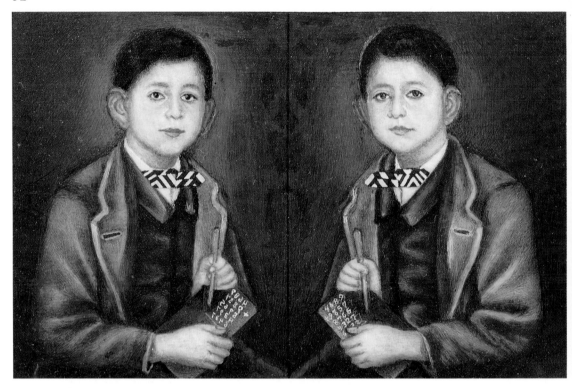

2

104

November 24th 4.17.14 m.   Shurs Gutman 1973

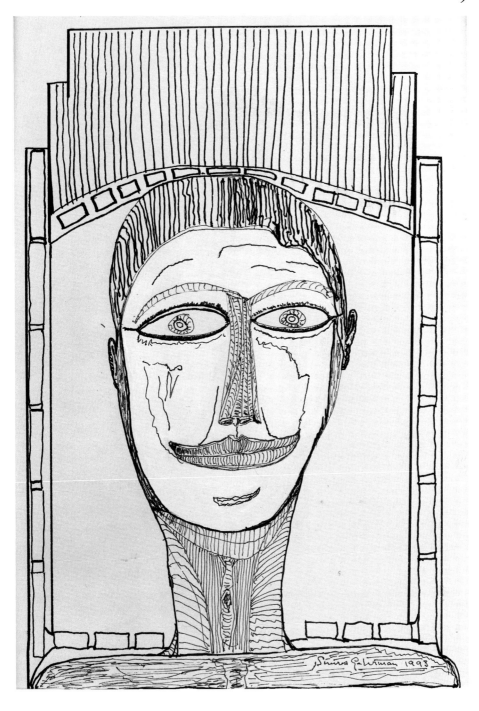

Sharon Goldman 1973

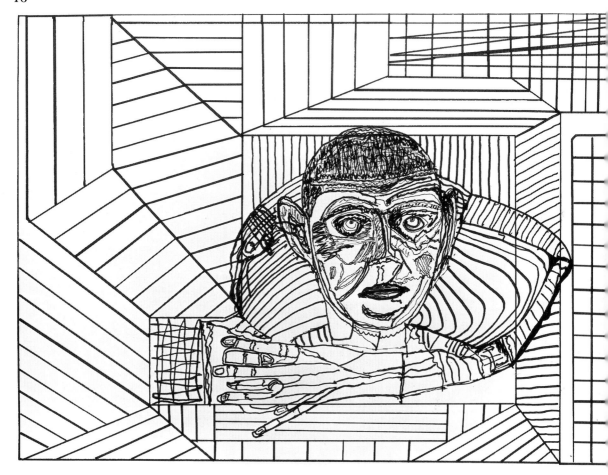

1993.

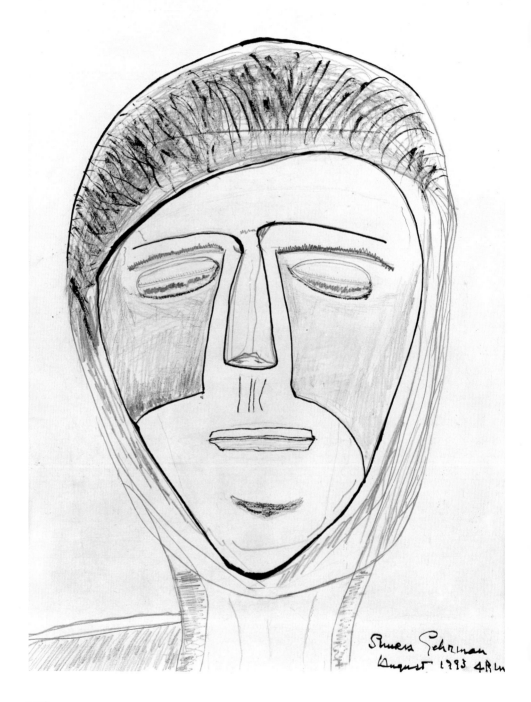

Shukru Gohrman
1973.

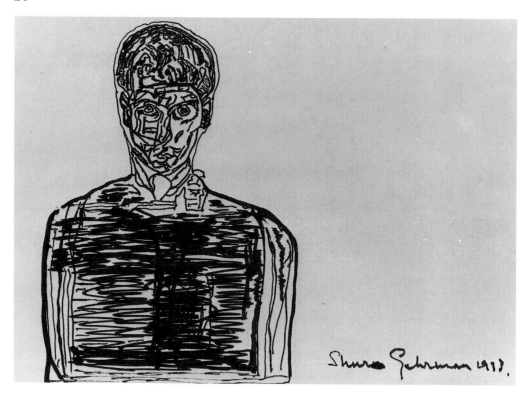

Shura Gehrman 1993.

The Man Who Steals the Flame

Let us suppose that the poet is the man who steals the fire, that he is responsible for humanity, even every animal that lives, has lived, will live. He must see that his inventions can be felt, smelt and above all heard. If what he brings back from his innermost mind has form, then he will bring forth form; if it is formless, formless it will remain. A new language must be found, for all words are signposts leading to an idea; the time of a universal understanding must come. All mankind will destroy itself if it cannot accept this concept. Only an academician, deader than a fossil, could fail to understand this. Feeble-minded people, who have not gone beyond the first letter of the alphabet, stray into the world without knowing the world. This new understanding would of course be of the soul, the spirit, the innermost mind; it should contain all things — smells, sounds, colours, thought transcending thought, latching through and pushing past the mind's barriers. The poet would measure the awakening of the all unknown in the universal noosphere of his own time, building on past words a bridge to the future time so as to produce a formulation of the march towards change. Guiding the enormity of mankind, being absorbed by everyone, he must be a multiplier for progress. This future has to become material, filled by numbers and harmony. These poems will be made to last. Essentially it will be Greek poetry awakened once again. Eternal art must serve a function since writers and artists are citizens. Poetry should rhyme with actions — it must be ahead of them.

Men like this will exist!

The first Romantics were seers not realising what they were. The cultivation of their souls they began without understanding of what they were starting and stopping, nor did the rest of mankind understand. The clues are there, they always have been and will be always, though we always refuse to see them.

The second Romantics have learned from their predecessors and are very seeing: Theophile Gautier, Leconte de Lisle, Theodore Banville. Examining the invisible and hearing the unheard-of is totally different from recapturing the spirit of things which are dead things, rehashing what has already been done. This means starting from nothing with nothing — precepts long finished are useless to repeat. Baudelaire is the great poet, a real one, although he lived in too closed an artistic group. To praise only the form which is most praised in him is to see him in very dim light indeed. Inventions from the unknown demand new life, and they will have it.

Most people are taught to see things wrongly and hear things wrongly from the beginning of their lives. Not all, but most accept without question standards given them. Not until mankind has devised a telepathy of ideas can we hope to find peace, or stop ridiculing that which is to be found outside our knowledge.

136

Collected Poems
Volume 1

22nd February 1984.

For Michael

1

You cease to come to me in the garden.
The paths of loneliness and suffering are gone.
The overgrown paths and trees hide your face.

It is evident that you no longer mind our loss.
The path which I tread to the shadowed church and graves means
    nothing any more to you.

It is enough that I watched you die slowly, as though you were
    going to sleep.
You no longer seek the shade which you so loved. Remember me
    when you awake.

Myself

2

Because I listen, I hear words, not truths.
I listen, in truth I can say the winds have stopped fighting
    and the leaves are silent now.
The church which I built in the fire dies with the dying fire.
I am no longer afraid —
Although I cannot sleep.

For Adrian

3

Will you sleep on the cold earth, and if so why?
The unchanging sky lights the eternal morning.
You think that you can retain your wisdom in this
    your profound life.
But beware, because your hands will tire of holding
    your childish pride.
Remember too that work well done will grow for you.

For Joy McArden

4

It seems that you know the two rivers —
The extreme sadness, the extreme joy.
There, through the grey roses of life you passed.
But I still think of you as eternal.

5

Wait till I join you
Keep away the cold winter world.
Sky, you are also menaced,
There is a precipice of hate in our home lands,
That is why we had to leave.

6

I love you mysterious souls
To find in each of you
My own soul.

7

Oh encounter, our wings fly
Side by side.
But what is it that shines above us?
The reflections of hope.
We lived in hope
That we shall not leave the world too plundered.

8

I know that I am being watched
I look at my death through the eyes of another
He loved me so well once
Look sleep the trees with their wide open branched arms.

9

See through the night he walks in the room.
What is this path that seems never finishing?
All through the night the boat seeks the shore.
What are these absent dreams? Are they a blessing?
What is this death that cures nothing?

The woman who fed cats by the sea
10

Kind was she, this dumpy woman with the warm eyes. She smiled
as she fed them. The cat family, they all came to her: they
were wild cats, mostly black. Some had several patches of
white; mostly black though. She goes there every day to do
this. A few people stopped to look. But they none of them
understood what she was doing.

She was a kind woman who fed cats by the sea.

8th March 1984.

11

He smiled at me. Perhaps he was about eight, I could not tell.
Smiling back, I said hello. He smiled again, one trouser leg in
his wellingtons. The warden and his wife frowned, for he was
falling back to smile at me. He waved joyously and I put my arm
on his shoulder. I do not think that he could speak. They had
walked by the sea. That moment we shared when he smiled at me.
This little boy with a bald patch among his fair hair smiled at
me.

12

The world of comfort sleeps on
In the delicious mirror of itself.
It does not see people die;
It does not listen to people cry
Nor does it see the young and old
Lie sleeping in passages that are cold.
The tired world has almost forgotten them as well.
How many times through all time has it seen its poor,
Both young and old — they who no longer have much hope —
Live or manage even to survive. Has it ever seen them?

13

The bird in flight separates itself from death
The wildlife in the fields nibble in the sunlight
They have forgotten all pain, all memories of it.
They do not know that tomorrow might not come for them
They are the blessed ones —
They have not been cursed.

2nd March 1984.

14

Is it possible when I drink in peace
My pain will allow it? — where is not important.
Shall I learn to be patient?
If I have any gold, shall I choose to keep it?
How shameful to think of this.
Or, if I should become my own vagabond,
Shall I miss the world that I renounced?

15

Do not yet call me a hollow man —
Although in truth I am. With grasping fingers
I do eat to fill this hollow silence of the mind.
The mind will kill me if it can.
Oh truths long forgotten, come back to me
To tell me what I am.

16

Everything flows with mysteries of old landscapes
Paid to be made by slave trades. Oh yes, our lands
Were paid for by this, it is not new to know this,
Just forgotten.
The voices of a hundred crows remind me
Of them — they used to throw the dying ones overboard, you know.
The wide movements of the trees whisper and remind me
Of this horrible thing — are we white with fear? and are they
      dark with anger?
Oh you large estates in your beauty, do you not feel the guilt
      of it?
The stronghold of power could never be called wholesome.

17

Beauty is sometimes a camouflage for deception. You will find
      this out. Simply listen.
Beauty is a concept, not a condition, and (like charm) if one
      becomes aware of it, then it no longer exists.

18

If you ask me why new love unlocks doors that I thought would
      not open for me
Now that I am old or nearly old —
The Gods have given me the gifts of love which I still hold.
I know this and that and that is that I love anew:
But love through this new love makes more love for the older
      love live new.

March 16th 1984.

19

Oh what fire in the planes of my mind
What pure shades in the amiable silence of the stars.
I look towards the coming day with its cold realities and I see
      that you are alone in your innocence dressed in mourning.

Listen to me and my dreams,
Let me take you to my present garden.
Abandon the night and its sombre shades.
Live for yourself to give to others
Your new loves and gifts.

20

All the night the beast moves in her cage, looking for her never
ending path home. We have torn her away for our pastime's
enjoyment, so merry to look upon. All in the name of science.
We cut and snip most mercifully, we are assured; there is no
pain, of course. What import are a few monkeys anyway? We are
assured again in the Bible, no less, that God made the beasts
for our use. Be absolved therefore, my children, all will be
forgiven you; all this maiming and hurting will after all give
our women better make-up.

All the night the creature shivers in her cage.

What is her death for? What is her suffering for? Well, my
best beloved, the men who club the new seals for their fur
assure us that this is a kindness. And they who kill the monkey
tell us it is after all needed to make women more beautiful.

What are these deaths doing to us?

Remember — we are quite good at killing men also.

21

All songs that sing reproach
All sounds that sigh lightly
Do not mean much if they are not meant rightly.
All the mighty men and all their mighty deeds
Are done for now
And mean nothing for us if they were not meant rightly.

22

— I could not rewrite this and listen to music.
When I was young I always listened to music's sounds
        when I wrote. But there now the time has changed for me

and I can no longer do this.
The ears of the mind have stopped me cheating.

23

In the useless habits of the great who go through life creating
what they must, living in past remembered things. They are
ghosts entrapped by not giving up the past.

Tintagel 1952

24

The sea cried
A sad purgatory for an entire land.
I have seen men weep for themselves,
And others die for others.
And at times there have been some crying mothers
Crying for their sons as lost lovers.
There are no new words for lovers,
There is nothing new for parting,
And sometimes eyes will seek a loving softly starting.
But light, light what return, what hand shall place the box
With withered rose leaves on granite's insubstantial rocks?
Now seatides polish sand anew on a forgotten land,
      as the gulls cry
Making sounds of fairground cardboard trumpets as they fly —
I know that I shall be my enemy before I die.

25

Night, and with our ticket's worth of life,
We drag incidentals sombre
Hate, pain, poison, blasted black.
No daybreak shall surrender, in darkness we remember
      only darkness,
Deeper thoughts that shake the sleeper sightless moving down and
      darker deeper. Night is only for the sleeper.

26

Just before dark, you sang your songs by the moon-striped sea,
And the words of your song blew into the perfect night.

Beautiful hawk night, is love the poor head that the plummet
    bird will crack?
Into my famined days soared a redeemer, and into the night
You plunged to kill with the terrible force of reason the
    feeble insight of yourself. You, the redeemer.
Go back to your pink cakes and parties.
There is no prescription to alter your destiny, if this is your
    destiny. I am the wilderness.
I could become soft, feminine, and take you for a time into the
    folly of the world and give you chocolates and say that you
    would never tire of my honey. But I have nothing of this
    for you, or honey.
Should I teach you to laugh at immense vulgarities? No, better
    not. Better forget that the world will always catch the
    noblest victims, the redeemer, to cast into the wax the
    misted future and give to the grave itself.

27

I remember, yes remember, when the night songs came so gladly
Never sadly would you sing them, as I listened to you say
All is but a moment. So let the moment stay.
I remember, yes remember, when the night changed to the day,
Calling me away. Then you let me go so gladly
As the night changed to the day.

28

Good and bad. Two ways of moving about your death by the
grinding seas. King of your heart in the blind day of your
reason, go crying through you and me and all the souls of men
into the innocent — the dark and the guilty dark, the good death
and the bad death — and then into the lost element fly like
stars' blood.

29

The dream is the form that is near. One to ten,
My footsteps pass again: then they pass fear, there is no fear
For fear is time and time's no longer here.
Just to wait, to wait and try again — it seems unwise to explain.

144

19th March 1984.

For René Ramond 1917–1943

30

This is hard. You have been dead, my dear. In our earth time
you have been dead for many years. You who taught me so much
when I was so young, my love. When you were alive I never even
thanked you for your smile that I have never forgotten. When
you died, my friend, I forgot your smile for a long time — froze
it out of me because I could not have you earthbound. Oh yes I
loved you. Like all the old, I reminisce. Now I can dare to
open the old wound. I must, you see — just to say thank you.
Remember we never said goodbye.

Your mother came for you when you were dead. She wanted to take
you away. She could not face to see you dead, my love, so much
my hidden love. She was not to blame for asking me to be by
your graveside when this was done. So I saw your dear dead face
with stubble on your chin. The simple words were quickly said —
Yes, that is he. I did not have the courage to tell them that I
loved you my friend.

17th March 1984.

31

Oh you sad world, why sadden me more? I have seen the earth
begotten and seen the skies looking down forgetfully at all of
us. We who grieve — we who wish for past remembered days which
we spent so freely — we who have loved too much, knowing all the
dangers of not holding back our loving, knowing knowing before
the inevitable loss of our beloveds — all this we knew, and
knowing knowing this, that in our weary world all our joys in
loving must die most surely, we still loved, and would still.

Now it is enough, I am still a child and like a child. Let me
go, release me. Let me, my thoughts both glad and sad be
extinguished — though just before, let me return all this loving
which I have loved. May I in the last knowing be thankful of
our meetings, and for all the love bestowed me.

The Desert

19th March 1984.

1

I walked amidst woods which seemed utterly filled by silence, as
if they breathed secretly, afraid to remind man that they existed.
And on that day, the wise winds respected their wishes for
silence, because they only whispered in their leaves. The plants
growing there would not betray them either. I became utterly
invisible; only your face in my mind looked upon me. The bees
feeding from the flowers made me aware that everything was still
living in the silent world.

We will separate — you living in the sweet pastures, the perfumed
lands of hope, I in the desert of my kingdom, knowing that all
things die. Feeling neither cold nor heat, I govern. Do not put
out your hand in friendship, for you would only find void. Could
you suffer that and not hate me?

At this time I laugh at the world, and the world returns my
laughter. In the times that have never existed, I govern: my
kingdom is of dust.

2

And not forgetting to pain's increase as well. There is no longer
any wish to see your beauty on looking into the waters which
shiver at your profound reflection. There is no more wishing left
in me, whether you remain joyous or become sombre in this world of
joyous wonder in the youth and springtime of your time. No one
can complete your crying, or wipe away your tears.

You lie sleeping peacefully, and the anchor which you lowered down
is well embedded in the river's sands. Pits of memory, oh heart

146

you do not let go, still fighting to regain the invisible solitude
of mine. Let your anchor lie embedded.

Underneath a low bower you sleep comfortably. Poet, be glad and
confident until you find your loss. The bridge, the chord which
link us will surely break.

My joys in loving begin anew, and loving things makes and takes my
journeying through into new lands of the mind's own lands, known
but never visited before. Spirit of love, these pastures of all-
seeing are wonderful. Forget for ever my goodbyes. Sleep and
awaken new, my friend. Pass into the realms of peacefulness which
I shall never know, into the innermost night. The dark is where I
am, so do not look, for there is nothing to see. Look past the
dark, for you will surely find your own morning light-time there.

3

Oh sweet death, wounded death, all solace gone. But somehow in
the autumn days, the days which come to us just before winter sets
and the trees shine in copper gold in the tiring sun, one
remembers — remembers travelling back to the past days that seem
to come from future time, now life's nearly done. Remember this,
that in every love there is seed for growing, and that through
loving there is always giving — nothing shopped for, understand.
The gesture of loving is giving, but giving only the love you
understand. In every right loving good grows, like a benediction.
You should know that love leads to loving more, and not forgetting
to pain's increase as well.

4

Reflections of this day in the calm water
    that only searches to recapture
    the love lost long ago
The pain of loss and of death so profound
    has returned
I do not dare know if it really is day
    or if I have the right still to love the shadow
    that troubled him in his high walled death.
My love remembered loves who now are dead.

A lighted torch is carried burning through the grey misted day
       to tear away its greyness for me
There is only the transparence of the flame to bring us light.
We shall walk hand in hand into the world's deserts
       and somehow the flowers will grow for us.

The sands, once fertile earth as earth started:
Man and time with hate tore up this continent, now every day the winds
       carve shapes in this once earth, in this now sand.
The horrible dust is blown into the cold night
You, you stars up there, why have you led us into this devastated land?
Why do we speak such vain words?
Better that we should walk along the sea sand shore
       and so adventure into another land, into another cold.

5

Often in the silence of the high hills
I hear — or wish to hear the silence of words
I sometimes see a bird which has died
       and which has fallen amidst the thick branches
Long and slowly did I suppose it took to die
This blind fall into death —
Will it be like that for us?

I think of the long procession of our lives
       into the country without birth or death.

6

The bird no longer sings, it cannot sing of miseries.
Where is the world's voice which promised truth and peace?
       Has it lied to us I wonder?
       and is it therefore dumb in silent shame?
It only sings now in pride and arrogance.
It only is capable of singing false praises to its dead —
       that they have murdered in their fine reasoning.

7

I have had little time to understand
       or to be. I have had little time to learn
       or to know. In hurt, in pain, in joy, in love

148

I know I am — and I thank the plural Gods —
   there cannot be just one.
I was shadow, shade and light
And I had patience to listen to silence
And I knew that the fires never burned in vain in me.

April 11th 1984.

8

Oh bird of ruined cities, you have separated yourself from our dying
You are no longer bound.
You nest in the seeming eternal clouds by the sun
You have thrown out all pains and memories forgotten
You do not know that your domain is eternal!

9

I am like the bread you eat,
Like the fire that you make
And like the stream which takes you
      to death.

Like the ever dying waves
      that continue dying for us,
Like the ever living light that guides us to port
Like the bird in the night flying into the night
Like night winds that shout havoc to us.

10

I loved you in silence — the rain song
      was all that I sang to you.
As your mother loved you — she must have,
      even in your wonderful mischief as a boy,
So do I. If the word loving means loving
      then loving let it be.

11

In the desert of my silence in the silence of my song
In the singing I have sung for you who might not understand
I tell you this, that that was right.
Pretty words, or pretty sounds, make nonsense of the song.

Collected Poems
Volume 2

14th April 1984.

1

I have danced where the soul has lived and have heard the spirits joyously, long ago when I was among you in your country, and that, oh of all remembered things I remember my completeness. Beings of my beings, souls of my brothers, where are you, for I do not understand your mystery — you are, are all things known past and in the unpast — impossible lover that I love, and my unbegotten son. You have taken form from me, and this I have given to you with all my loving love. I have broken into the silent waters of your peace from time to time. Traitor though, your name is my name. I must believe that you love me when you tell me this. I do not understand why I fear your hurting me, for pain is not new to mortals. My joy is yours and my heart lies in your unknown eyes. My gifts, both bad and good, are my only fruits which I give. And as my passage through this world passes, it is from my songs I go journeying into you.

2

Into the dark passages and pleasures of the night we ride forth; in the dark pleasures, which we find dark doors to open, that show us anything and whatever one may wish. Beware, this is but dreaming the dream, in total distortion of truth. The God that we were taught to pray to is nothing but a reflection of our own vanity: the God, the sublime one, which in all our names we call upon for help, deserts us, whatever ritual or sacrifices you make or observances you do. In this world and our huge pain, the God our God and mighty God, who made us in seven days, so the fools said and wrote — and now listen to this, they believe it — should

150

look down at his supposed handiwork and weep in shame!

And we the complacent ones should be wiped away.

3

Fortune dwells in our own heart, for in us dreams live that shall
ever outlive our world's sadness and the evil that we see amidst
the trying good that shall always wreck the small empire of our
vain hearts and our short time here. Do not please be unwise, so
unwise not to hope for peace — the right peace and the true peace
of those who have come before us, and they who will replace us as
our time ends in this the only path which we see.

22nd April 1984.

4

Deserting dead ashes, he looks at their grey death
And he remembers that his eyes once, not long ago, saw them aflame,
Bright and living things with the impatience of life.
He forms with his hands a cathedral full of sombre windows which
     throw away their light to become dark and sober shades.
He has torn away for ever the rose life of the flamed curtain.
He knows that his awakening has begun, and that the very bones of
     the Earth are shaking in their fear.
There is nothing but to start his journeying now. The Earth
     forgets nothing, watches all doings, and for ever sighs
     at new follies as well as old.
He is journeying in his new days, in his new life. Quickly the
     memory of his past fades from him, leaving only faint
     resonances of the past for him ever again. Newborn and
     unremembered lives slip away from his remembering.
He is grave in his efforts. His grey silver face seems still,
     though, to remember fire.
He touches a small vein, and bites it open with his sharp teeth,
     to feel the pain — but the grave cold only leads him to the
     passion and violence of making another fire.

5

Through the gates of heaven the serpent creeps, and passes through
the secret stones and the grasses as easily as anywhere, and as
simply as she does in hell.
This pallid gliding creature sheds doubts among us all. Laugh at
them and think harder for yourselves. Pick up her shed dead
skins. Crush them. These are your doubts, my soul. Although
remember, doubts can bring forth good if your doubts are not
fearful ones.

6

She did not live in my country.
She came on a visit to see me.
She came, and because she was my mother, I turned away. I had no
     time for her demands then.
She was old, but I did not seem to notice that.
She was ill, but I did not see her illness.
I prayed that she would return home and leave me.

She left me all right, and that through her dying. I did not know
that she was dying. They told me so in hospital one Saturday
morning. I did not like my mother, Blanche, and I foolishly did
not know that I loved her still so much. She kindly waited for my
visit before dying. I took hold of her hand. Never believe that
people in coma have no knowledge of what is happening. I comforted her,
and by pressing my hand she comforted me.

She died well, and, as a child, I cried for her return as only a
child can.

24th April 1984.

7

Nighttime girl of sorrows which you cannot change
The grey room, peaceful in its choice of greyness, a choice for
     consolation perhaps,
And the heart in its calm fever of love lives on throughout her
     long deserted night.

152

We must watch very well this dead face that she so loved — it has
   in no way changed as yet in death. The lines of his troubled
   face are still there: they will dissolve soon though.

On the table the single large-flamed candle whispers as it burns.
   The turns of its wick seem to try to retain its own life as
   the wax melts.

Calm shades of night, take his poor face to your unknowing
   shadows,
Colour slowly her grief with peace without telling her.

8

Oh what hurt in the pain of the lost,
What shame. But the stars in their silver silence simply continue
   to wink back their own deaths, and amid the dark sheets of
   water they are reflected back into their own void.
You are alone in the dark and invisible night. Why do you
   continue to stand there, and what awaits you in your constant
   vigil? You pale statue, who remembers your living?

9

Wait for me until I return,
Send away the cold people who separate us.
Clouds, in your high halls, disband your dark shadows
   to let in the light.

10

Oh you privileged ones who bask in sunlight and the clean clear
   winds, who dip their fingers into the soil, the clean earth,
You are the privileged ones whom the Earth has not ravaged, nor
   made you cry havoc!

11

Abandon the joyful box of the world,
The play boxes, the fun boxes, throw them out.
These young people who have never smiled at anything but for their
   own pleasure,
The jealous ones who demand to be loved for ever, who have not

learnt really to love.

Love is teaching and being taught anew every day. Love is loving
when you go away.

Do not think that brown eyes or blue eyes matter much at all, or
the beauty of the hair — it is the strength of the soul that
will be your life raft in the turbulent water wall breaking
the spirit of your young heart in this world's false promises
and promising ways.

25th April 1984.

12

Yet again this perfume which enflames me
A new time for looking at beauty
and listening to your great flames of sound.
In the far off distance the dance of time shines clearly —
A new finding, a new return, a new greenness.

Nothing but the drunken light of twilight could release you
in your beauty of truth.
The sun knows that you become more beautiful
in its burning ray of daytime,
And the new nights will cull their violets for you to hold.

Oh my desires in springtime are joyous,
One cannot sleep without dreaming.
Your thoughts take me completely, and to think of your love
shatters my spirit.
To each one of us some day comes music
The enchantment of April seems to become life
And the words I think make me adore the greening new leaves
of living unforgettable beauty, forgetting its own beauty.

Glad people who come to love each other
Follow your paths that mirror the ephemeral times of love,
Pass through the secret gardens where the soft winds blow
to your madness the scent of golden roses.
Listen for ever to the singing of the invisible birds.

154

For Barbara

13

Your kitchen when I came to see you was clean, it smelt good. By the way, I have not forgotten that the meal which you cooked for us was good. But then, your quiet dignity and your patrician walk and ways, and how you set about preparing it, should not have surprised me that it was going to be good. Your face is mostly always calm, or so it would seem, and the clean fine hair added the reassurance of calmness — although I never did stroke it to find comfort. No, that comfort came from your quietly smiling eyes with their assurances of good; and so simply you gave me your friendship and your smile, I hardly knew it was there. That you were not happy at that time, seventeen years ago, or so it seemed to me, was better not to mention to you.

8.27 a.m., 6th May 1984.

14

Oh sad fate of women, that you seem to have to look always young for us men. Do not mind, but try to forgive us our boyish foolish hungers. Never forget that your real beauty is within your selves. Scorn men who only want to slobber over your young and soft skin and who make love to it and to your womanhood so that when you are defenceless in your excitement you betray your innermost being. Turn away from the men who debase you.

Oh women, I do not like most of you because you try too hard in many of your cunning ways to please, to make us lecherous. Many times through your scorn you unman us. Make us love you by not holding on too hard to us. Do not expect that some of us will not love others than yourselves. Do not be surprised that you too will find others who will give you comfort and other harbours as well in your living.

To have and to hold from this day onwards, and to forsake all others, is another of our mother church's damned blasphemies. Remember, you bear our crying children, but we must share the smells, the loving and the frustrations which, when we so wish to do, we so easily slip away from, because we have other things to do. What about you? Have you nothing else to do? Love your children, but remember not to forget yourselves, in spite of marriage or no marriage. You must survive as well. The last secret I tell you is that I have seen real beauty in older women who have fulfilled themselves. You need never trouble yourselves about anything sagging. You are real, and you are the eternal flame of life. Homage.

My friend, I love you. So do not talk of how beautiful you find a woman's bottom is; do not ever say again to me, 'I need a woman'. After all, you are still young, as I was. But remember you can wipe away your destiny like this. You are made of fire to love with and a nature which warms the soul's spirit. Do you want to become one of the ever searching cold stoney-eyed men whom you must have already observed?

Remember that in ten years' time there will be new and other beautiful bodies for your delight, and that the ones which made you breathless will by then start to sorrow as they begin to sag.

6th May 1984.

15

Kind lady in blue, kind lady in blue, I do not very much like you. Are you the best dragon that we can find to defend us? That you once went to the length of getting a degree does not mean very much to me. Stop to think — that is, if you can feel what thinking is, of course — that in one of your silly utterances you called yourself a scientist; wonder of wonders, a chemist! And low we bowed down to you, our now second Queen! If you should decide to rule us again, choose men, not faceless fools who dance — perhaps not the tango, where you so rightly met your match at the *thé dansant* — but certainly the slow foxtrot, to the tune of Reagan's Dance of Death.

Eyes to a Distant Horizon

11.30 a.m., 6th May 1984.

1

The dog that cries and howls
    trembles about his feet.
The magic wisdom has suddenly left him,
The bewitching enchantment of his life has departed.
No more running, no more catching the fleet flight and power.
Now that it is no longer there and has stolen all of his loving habits,
    something tells him that it is time to die.

2

Song bird of my sadness, of my insufficient definitions,
Your song is my fragment
And your wings have destroyed my life's fortunes.
But unlike you I cannot fly.

3

These people who appear in their coldness, demanding wars and the
    firing of guns to kill us — the jailers who keep the cages ready
    for us so that they may continue to murder, are impostors that we
    shall with the world's anger destroy.

4

Sleep in the cradle of my hands and arms,
Lift up your young eyes in trust, trustingly,
So that the slender stems of hope will support you
    when you are alone in your black despair.
Carry into your night all of your gentle loving
And love in quiet peacefulness and silent music.

5

The lark simply sings, surprising us that she is already awake,
Awakening us.
Oh secret wishes to hear yet again your song have surprised me anew.
Go flying. Go singing. Go away.

6

Dear shades which we become in the calendars of our years,
Give us our flowers, give us our comforts,
And let this our last loving, our hands comforting hands,
Comfort the world in all its torment.

7

The heart that responds to the river's call and the clearness of its
waters will carry me to the infinite water of the seas. I can no
longer ignore the surging calls that I listen to, for I have become
suddenly curious to know your immutable mysteries.

8

Pain and time melt together in time.
Why do they thus assemble?
Take your flight, my beloved birds,
And fly away if you can from the sad and weary nothing of our world.
Your blue skies and horizons are so much better than ours,
my lovely creatures.

9

Thank you, death. Why are you so astounded?
Thank you, death, for not insisting just yet.
Thank you for simply another day.
Thank you for making me a simple man, and thank you
for being a god.
We shall meet again, always I hope in friendship.

Collected Poems
Volume 3

3.42 a.m., 7th May 1984.

1

I touch you, and as your body breathes
I understand that these are not the times for us to lead
    separate lives.
Your coming to me on that quiet day, for good or bad
    has rebuilt my world.
Although I have still never felt further away from my joy,
I am in joy.

2

Gather together together our treasures,
These marvels, these serious pleasures
And absolute colours.
I find you are still asleep, and when I whisper very gently to you
You do not know of my farewells, you do not hear.
Like the dead goodbyes of the past,
You do not hear them.

3

Your sleep is very deep, and the complete silence is broken only
    by its rhythm. You were in my arms, in total peacefulness,
    but I never forget that I was alone. To be nearer to one's
    own mysteries is no answer for knowing them.
Like a man playing with fireworks, I never know when their colours
    will vanish.

4

The day which attacks our loveliness
Renders it more touching and more beautiful than itself,
And its shades and the guard of its strange perfumes
     are my essences of calm.
It is like the greatest comfort and blessing.
The day reborn, and the night is still with us
With the calm greyness of giving up its dark.

5

You sleepy houses and fields, fold again your arms among us for
     another few hours. Keep us away from our troubled lives a
     little more time.
My song may I think of and never sing it again. My skies are my
     sadness, and my despairing of ever hearing words of
     reassurance again.

6

Like the seashells echo the sea sounds,
My mind weeps with mad remembered sorrows.
I tremble when I take you to my heart's garden lest you should
     laugh at my flowers
And take away in one careless cast of words our good loving,
And tell me only of its dangers
     of which I am only too well aware.

7

Oh my love, the time is flying away.
A thousand and one days and nights are never enough for lovers.
Take this love for a day, for a lifetime,
Take the flame.
Be careful that it does not burn itself up as a stubble field, and
     by so doing burn up the magic carpet
Which brought us to our loving.

8

What new frights will you bring me now?
What are you looking for in my perpetual storms?
As the time flies away, never to return,
Are my years finished already?
The years mount up, my friend, you do not have the time you think
      you do. I know, because I thought just as you do. There is
      not enough time for everything.
Oh, what hope is trampled upon by useless doings.
Take away all my wastes of time and the foolish messages of folly
So that I may live out my time in love and work.

4.36 a.m., 7th May 1984.

9

I recognise this statue of the dancer in stone, holding her ever
      still robes and her tambourine immobile.
What makes her come to seeming life in the night-time's moonlight?
She is awake. She slowly rubs open her stone eyelids. Her beauty
      is for ever.

      I should have fixed in my memory this mauve-grey rose light which
      was until then unknown to me and unseen before.
Oh you phantom domino, fixed and moving along the deserted avenues,
You never will have need to change your dresses.

4.47 a.m., 7th May 1984

10

I seem to stop some people from thinking, and they are shocked at me.
      I trouble their sleep. God knows I have no remorse at this.
It appears also that I give some people disquiet —
      the Nice people and the false people, that is.
That my anger could only awaken the dead and rework their dreadful
      past deeds — that would please me.
The time is 4.54 and 45 seconds and I have just heard the first
      morning rising birdsong.

11

Where to begin. 'A vast desire awakes and grows unto forgetfulness
of thee', to quote Yeats. But in my case, not into forgetfulness, but
awareness — awareness that my life was mine and that somehow a great
journey had begun for me.

12

Oh you simple words, why are you the hardest to say and accomplish, or
try to accomplish? Youth, love, flowers and loving should never die.
Yet these are the first things we always try to kill in ourselves and
in others. Watch a child destroy — perhaps a toy — perhaps on a sunny
day of flowered wonder. They are quite simply able to plunder the
woodland flowers and after a few moments throw them out without any of
their fulfilment. Is it because they have never been told not to do
so, or is it that in their young lives Death has already called them
to his secret palaces and shown them how to kill?

11 p.m., 12th May 1984.

13

A new time for this incendiary perfume
A new time for the caresses which are carried from the air
A new time finding yourself bewildered and astonished to know yourself
    glad in the renewed renewing.

Queen of all the twilights, pale as the moon in the summer-still nights
    of reflection with all passion thankfully spent,
Renew our palettes with better colours this time,
So that in the long nights we can gather your beautiful violets and
    pay you better homage than our shared lusts.

The desires of spring play in us
We can no longer sleep peacefully without our dreams of romance
The insurmountable days of false loving insist on our loving them
    and so much burn out our spirit — sometimes for ever.

To each of us our music speaks
The enchantment of April surrounds me
And oh, the sweet tender words which I remember,

162

The sad promises which must be broken so that I may remember truth
Although I find to my dismay that your perfumes can still destroy me.
Unforgettably, I must forget you,
     my Queen of my tormenting twilight dreams.

No words are too grand or too mad when they are meant for you.
Your light pours down on me like vast rainbows which are, I suppose,
     your jewellery, presents of your loving.
Oh you birds which are able to fly in all the sky's colours,
I envy you so much.
In your skies there lie countries vast and for ever unknown.

Miseries which I cannot name —
In this misanthropic time which hates much more than loves,
I plead that if these mad badnesses be placed into your so loving
     hands which are gentle,
They would vanish and plague us no more.

14

I walked through and amidst the wooded land,
The land heartbroken and hardly breathing.
Even its plants had no memories.
The mountain lifted itself full of great warning and lit by shadows
That seemingly wanted to swallow all about itself into invisibility.
My traces and my existence are lost,
Your face slides away from my memory the more I try to remember you.
It was only a fool that made me sad
And that fool was me. You are gone.

11.30 a.m., 16th May 1984.

15

How much suffering does the world have to bear to become the
habitation for man, and to fashion itself to man's wishes which are
made in turns between the pages of a book, man's machine? That it
must be made spectacular or extravagant for the importance of making
the writer important — covering over the deep fissures of ignorance in
order to propagate the myth of man's grand importance to himself,
which has to be pursued at all costs. Trying to fight for the
simplest smell of truth causes man much distress. No no, that cannot

be allowed at all — that would be childish and not right. Death lies
in his sleeping with this delusion, but no matter. Stop taking the
branches for the trunk and the roots of life's trees — this might just
become for you a beginning.

16

Sure that by myself I am waiting for my sorry courage to return,
Sure that by that precise time I shall not be courageous enough
      to stop hurting my heart or wounding it. As sure as I know
      these things, I surely know that these pains cannot be avoided.
Less and less I cry of love which haunts me in the night's day
      when I still feel your flames.
Cry, crying into the city which is also burning, although the city's
      flames are different — they spring from the garbage of the mind
      and dust and dirt of the body.
What is the use of shouting beware to sleepwalkers and the sleeping
      dead?
To cry out my loving from day's aubade is useless to the blind or
      to the deaf. Searching searching, where are you my beloved eyes,
      have you gone blind as well in this dreadful city?
I remember the eyes with all their loving, and believe that I shall
see them again.

17

The night which lives in the heart and comes from it will never know
      or see the morning of day.
Another light, an inverse one, will light that masquerade
Beneath black mimosas which, with their pollen falling,
      smudge its pale white leaves.
Give to the faded gardens of the towns at least some room and air
      to breathe; do not suffocate them, or others, or yourselves.
Fly away if you can and if only from time to time from the damnable
      city, although remember that the flowers cannot uproot themselves
      like you. They lie in the ground in which they were planted,
These flowers that look like immobile dancers,
These people who breathe in the putrid air.
Cities were not always thus.

18

The carnival images of so-called loving. Abandon these things, they
have no roots in the good earth. They have taken root, the sad ones,
in the ever sifting soft gravel sands which the winds of quick life
throw away. They must be blown away.
Do we keep postcards — perhaps a few collectors do. No; we keep
letters though, very nearly all of us do.
Oh night at midday, you cannot eclipse any might of true country's
light or comparative peacefulness. They are less carnival images
where the trees and the true flowers grow in the good and quiet deep
earth. These cities' dirty flowers are no better or worse than
postcards, which we send unthinkingly simply 'to keep in touch'.

17th May 1984.

19

The rising sun ever growing
        forgetting how cruel yesterday
        replying to its sadness by quickly dying into the comfort
                of the night
        is already throwing its sinister shadows of passing lifetimes away.

20

Take your chance, forget about symbols of luck
        and run towards your fearful risks.
They will welcome you if you are not distracted on the way.

21

At the storm's strongest power, just look up.
You will always see an unknown bird flying towards its destiny.
We more often than not are very afraid of ours.

22

Fly away to search for the new young saplings.
Trees are always needing time to replace themselves.
After all you do have a forest of time to replant.

23

Build an arbour —
Build a simple roof,
Build the walls with wide arches
    so that the birds can fly joyously through them.
The windows must be of matching proportion,
    there must be unity — forget doors.
There must be a mirror, a vast one
    to show the world to itself.
It must be there also to show the flowers of my discontent.

24

Listen to the parting. Look at it also.
From your pride, so long for you to acknowledge,
The bucket of grain which you think will never rot
Has already defeated you by germinating.

25

Batter of sunlight, you clouds obscure like some dreadful city
    kills the land upon which it was built for profit, not
    for people.
Are you satisfied, you, you the dead men who plundered the
    farm lands of the land to make money and people sad?
What is your reply to this, you vile men?

26

Diligently we walk through our eternal grief.
You sad lonely people who pretend to be busy
You have done nothing with your lives except trouble those of us
    who try to do something.
Damn you and the bad advice of caution
    which you always seem so very pleased to give us.
Us, the makers. You, the destroyers.
What is accomplished, matters. But more than that is the trying,
    the searching.

166

27

Here in the light clean air it is no longer morning,
It is already daytime, full daytime
        with its loud clamouring for attention to its desires.
These memories, or mirages of songs in your memory's dream — these
        will remain.

Hear always here, stone upon stone
We shall always steal and take back our truths
        which are stolen from us by the world.
Just to listen to the falling full grown fruits from their trees
        reforms our nature.

28

Hurt me no more today, or tomorrow. I shall throw no more bombs
        at you ever, though remember that by repeating my silence
        and smiling and encouraging you at your distractions I am not
        your friend, and I become a coward — however many other things
        there are to do which I must do. Remember — remember,
                remember
        I loved you.

                                                        20th May 1984.

        29

Remember that all the golden beams of sunlight cannot comfort people
who mourn their dead. The tranquility of passing time does that. The
hurt and never healing wound of loss grows less very slowly. Beware
of not understanding this in your wonderful summertime and youth.

        30

What use of exile — for I cannot forget your bright colours, try as
you like to hide them in your secret crevices of dislike of men.

I would have liked to fix in my better seeing and knowing your
knowledge, but I only managed to understand a little of what you said
and taught me. Forgive me my hurting, but I knew no better then.

These balconies decorated in bronze ornaments, the rooftops green copper coloured, the light shining through onto them — and when you told me to sing Fauré like that, I then did not understand what you meant. The Emerald beautiful was a green I could not translate into the right sound or colour then — the sound cool as water, and as yet hot with passion, which must be made when you sing 'Mirage'. You were right; but I was thinking of the next time I would be meeting you. Who you were is now long forgotten.

I should have fixed in my mad memory your roselit wisdom. But I was running after domino phantoms along the glittering avenues, which excited me by their ever changing faces, words, deeds, and clothes to entrap me — which they did. But in the morning time all their bright colours and all their earnest promises had been no more than pale ashes.

The firmament carries diamonds for you. I play my heart for you in the hope that you can fly away from fool's gold and the cracked pavements that we have all to walk on, and the quick false lovings which are terrible to behold and terrible to know. You cannot afford cheap magic tricks in this world. Shall we never find our lost paradise which gave us peace?

2.15 p.m., 21st May 1984.

31

He comes, but his gestures are fixed,
    as are those of a statue.
He speaks, and his words belong to the language and empire
    of the dead.
He plays and acts softly, as though to please those
    whom he might need in the future.
He is already feeling the dead hand of wanting to be great —
    and by wishing for this, shows his utter foolishness and loss.

He smiles with true beauty playing on his face. The lamp that burns in the country of the dead and the vain has already shown itself to him. Through his strength and vanity unknown to himself, he lives in great danger. He protects himself quite wrongly by his own will. He wishes to be alone, so in his beautiful folly and vainness he proclaims this secret; and soon nice people will surround him because he is beautiful now and needs comforting. He will be comforted, have no fear. He need never worry again — he will be comforted. I wonder if he knows the price he must pay for this wonderful folly?

I can surely and will not or could not help him with his utter vain foolishness, although I do love him. What a pity, what a shame, what a dreadful waste, to waste his golden light; but I fear that it might be far too late already.

12.19 a.m., 25th May 1984.

For Youra Guller

32

Now in the hourglass perfection of time do I see the reflection
    of my time long ago.

Queen of all silence, Queen of the everlasting sand oceans that sang
    their sirens' song so long ago, come to me again just to remind me
    of my beginning, so that I shall remember you again and not be
    angry at myself for not knowing your very familiar face — my face
    so long ago.

To know that I was, and in strange ways still am and yet am no longer,
    is so cruel. The memory fades away before it's made, as soon as I
    think of remembering my past glories and my downfall.

The Journey

1.47 p.m., 25th May 1984.

1

The voice of he who has destroyed us still rings and sounds
    in the marbled forests of fear,
The footsteps which pass through an ordinary door in order to
    escape the night are softly dying in their feeble echoes in
    time.
Where does he come from? Where is he going?
Meanwhile, whilst we wonder these imponderables, he has won by a
    form of goodness which remains almost invisible — and only by
    the fragrant scent do we sense that he is present here.
The Sphinx cannot be more bewildering to any of us in time and
    countless grains of sand than his wonderful memories which
    he has given us to keep.
This is our day, our time. The countless times of universe are
    his minutes — oh, loving, loving is to hurt again
    remembering this.

From a picture of the mind, I take my time, I look and sing and
    walk through the sadness, and those who do not understand
    the droning hurdy-gurdy man in his past songs of misery
    are fools who bow at conceit as she passes smiling, bedecked
    by jewels and stones for the world to fawn at.
I sing for the sadness and the sorrows and the joys of this world.
I sing not to impress men nor women, I sing not to shock,
I sing to try and teach — how colours change, and fragment by
    fragment they turn into a firmament — that is why I do it.
And damn bel canto, these are tiny churches' tinny liturgies
    for me not to sing about.

11.10 p.m., 26th May 1984.

2

The day searching for its lost past
The water under the bridge is ever changing,
Changing towards the past
It tightens its prudish arms wide open
And all is lost in the joyous comfort of an infantile death.

It cannot say that it is really daytime
It cannot say the day is come
It still has a right to like the twilight dying night that has for ever
    opened the unwelcome fact of yet another morning light.

Let us make and carry a burning torch towards the greying morning
Let the fire brand tear into life this unwelcome day
There is only the fact of the bright flame,
Souring another empty day to make us hope.

3

I had a little time to understand and for being.
I was shadow that I liked to hide in, and I liked
    to guard my privacy.
I waited in great patience in great halls and rooms
    which did not belong to me,
        but I knew that your fire never burned in vain.
So that although I was a stranger in the land,
    you made me welcome for a time there.

4

The fire has caught all the branches of destiny
It will touch the heart, it will touch to its peril the frozen cold.
He that lives at the door of all things which are dead or dying
    must choose death to burn him.

But he knows it burns in pure loss.
In spheres' time, fire burns itself out.
The stars in the dark night will outlive all our fires,
The stars of the dead stars will lighten our path.

They will continue to watch over us,
We who live in night time's limits
    will know its passing in the coldness of the night.
The idea that we are not masters of our fate frightens us so much
        that we can often run into our worst disasters,
            and renounce our meant fate.

Collected Poems
Volume 4

5 a.m., 27th May 1984.

1

In your presence I come nearer to my peacefulness. You who have
made my sad mind mad with havoc — mad. In my days of rest, of
pain and work which I do, all I do is think of you through
everything I do. I have loved before, but never to be able to forget
you seems almost impossible to bear. But what can I do, turn away
from you? I should be ashamed to do that. And you my friend, do
you suffer this as well, in any way? If you do, we must learn
from it. Be closer for a time till the seas are still before we
take our departure of each other. I promise not to forget, but
give me peace from this raging hurt, it is very hard to support
all my waking hours in this hurricane of force. My eyes have met
your eyes and my spirit seems to have reached yours. It is as
though the tearing away of ourselves from each other is at the
moment impossible. If you do not suffer this, then I am glad.

Oh you grey stones, is it possible to cool my mind and blood from
this torment, or do I have no other choice? Open your doors of
pain for me so that we are able to hear each other's crying.

In this ravaged landscape, in this iceberg land, my mind and spirit
have become frozen in the howling winds. Give me a sign that we
shall be able to part from each other many times, to live not
quarreling, so that when we meet again we can love each other more
in our total acceptance of our love and fate.

2

Nothing can reunite this vast globe, this vast sunset of the desert by the burning sun very quickly burning itself out into the darkness. Soon the stars which seem pickable for me to give to you for no other reason than I wish to do so will be there in their clean coldness, in their diamond hardness.

What little importance are men's travellings if they miss the mind's adventure. There is the true world, there in the mind, not in the shops, ships or planes. There is where we really grow, and our voyages are worthwhile in time back and forth through this world.

Long for such dreaming nights which give us our true passages to love in this sombre shadow world, all too shabby with its cheap delights of today.

5.35 a.m., 27th May 1984.

For Kathleen Ferrier

3

All kindness and all irony melt. I say goodbye to your pure crystal voice which is made of twilight gold, which disappears into the misted shades of your death and of your dying. You with your grave shining eyes that I remember so well. All the world said that it knew you. But we in our silence know better. It is too easy to tell you that I miss you. Sing for me again in my mind. But I'm sure that now you have other songs and words which are too good for me to hear. Your songs are now really much more than we poor mortals could bear. My dear, thank you — it seems not enough to say, and yet too much.

Perhaps now I can say goodbye to you. I have no more tears and you have long ago flown away, my dear friend. But that voice, let me ask you for its memory a little while longer.

174

4

The mourning I think is well hidden,
    rather like a frightened bird just having escaped being caught.
Say if you like that this season of green spring time is not for
    mourning in, my reply would be, Why not? There is surely
    joy sometimes in winter time as well.
Why do you talk in the name of reason unreasonably,
    about such finite things which are infinitely more than finite?
What unknown dance will drag you away from your self this time
    yet again? You must put down roots, you are so afraid of
    them that soon you will persuade yourself that you no longer
    need any.
Break with nonsense and have courage.
Remember, I will not blame you if you fail; most of us do.
    There is, alas, only a very narrow gate to pass through —
    and that is only opened to you once.

12.49 a.m., 28th May 1984.

5

Tyrant nightmare reborn comes again to taunt me —
    it awakens my heart from its subterranean calms,
    it unchains my forgotten echoes of all that was harmony.
Other nights and other panics make their appearance to me again,
The forbidden word reappears in the whispering air to taunt me.

The lovely bodies of the young tremble in their own awareness. If
    you listen very quietly you can hear the young crying in
    their bewilderment. The world is not what they expected at
    all; they are nearly all of them unprepared. They can
    already hear the talking of old men and women — these corrupt
    ones, the embalmers of youth. My country forbids these
    people to rot or spoil the young. We cannot and will not
    bury and kill our future. Courage, and being only guided to
    your selves, is the only currency you need for your passport
    to your own strength. Never listen to fools who ask you if
    it is wise; and never underrate the need of utter right
    commitment. You are not a sleepwalker going into the

night time's doom of waste or of indulgence. Tomorrow will
not do today's work for you — but beware the wrong advice.
Do not be trapped by the familiar honeyed words which can
most times lead you to nothing other than void!

10.30 a.m., 28th May 1984.

6

The sea comforts, the sea takes away:
My sad eyes, why were you born sad?
My sad world and all the sadness contained in yourself, and that
    if all the seas were full of joy, grief would most surely
    drown them from all their crying rivers of painfulness
    falling down the rivers of hurt, pain and anguish throughout
    the world of woe. You foolish people who smile
    simperingly and scream, enjoy yourselves while you can:
    do you not understand why this is blasphemy? Do you not yet
    know, you withered men, that by your killing and raping and
    greed, by your arrogance, you are utterly damned by all the
    kind Gods, who care not at all for your puny powers —
    although your puny powers seem to be held here in my world
    in the highest esteem by blind and enfeebled people who are
    afraid to offend the filth which you are, lest you just might
    trouble them, or hurt them even. If only they understood
    that you are phantoms and hauntings, that if they let the
    light pour down upon your lying words and actions you would
    surely crawl away in your great disgrace and havoc.

In knowing love and loving and always learning better how to love,
    learning that sad lesson that loving cannot make or take
    away my utter being alone. That I should be and am loved
    is utterly wonderful to me, although I cannot understand why
    or know how they who do love me do.

In the garden that I sometimes walk in, I see the flowers and the
    fruits in their time and season give themselves up seemingly
    without any trouble or woe. I do not know of any way of not
    being alone in the deep seas of my own being.

7

All too late, my faded friends.
You have vanished into the night time of obscurity by simply
   telling yourselves that you must not be pushed because you
   are not ready. You simpletons, do you not understand that
   no one is ever ready for the birth of awareness, for the
   great leap into the black mirror from your sentimentality
   to your senses. Thrash your minds into wakefulness, you
   silly sleepers and dreamers of your own youth — as though it
   will continue for ever. Remember that you will be quite old
   at 25.

1.15 a.m., 29th May 1984.

8

Say thank you to death, and it is astounded. Say to death, 'Wait a
   while', and you will find that death will not always insist,
   but wait for you to find him. He is not always unkind to us.

Thank you when the tiresome days are finished. Thank you simply
   for being a man that holds in his hands, and giving me the
   comfortable peace of his kingdom for a time.

1.48 p.m., 7th June 1984.

9

The house trembles, and the dust leaves of memory vanish
   into the forgotten land.
The door is open
   and the shaken world returns,
   an outcast from the universe.
The sorrowful men unload all impersonal and outward observances.
Take up yet again all your burdens that bring sorrow
   after the easy crying is done.
The road grey with morning is open, and the moon is dead.

10

There on the soft rock — begun, begun
The world to itself
Spins as it spun, it sees the waves
Kill themselves, one by one.
Is there time to save you and me,
As we sit in our hollow to dig our grave?

The girl unbound sits by the water and counts the waves — seeing,
Seeing the long grey sea move, listens and stays,
Plaits her hair and prays in the melting mirror of her world.
At daytime a woman I knew turned her broken eyes and sought my hand
Lying, trying to comfort her sighing,
The rattling breath stopping her crying
Told me to stop away from the dying
The frown of old life on her face
Suggesting the final embrace.

11

Slowly swinging, the pendulum cut the edges of the moon, and the
white light lit the whole country of the sky, and the star columns
were slender. I walked by the moon's river that flowed in total
silence of glass that mirrored your face until I fractured the
surface with a stone.

I crossed the road again, my feet were cut by the tarmac. My eyes
were blind, and my fingers used themselves groping in the dusty
wastes of the world.

The wilderness completes itself and gives me back my eyes, but
when I saw the dry empty land, I cast out all my visions. Night
came and locked me in sleep.

All is a dream I tell you, there is nothing to understand when
everything is said, finished and done. Perhaps out of the dream
there is love, but love has always to live in impossible homes
with all the doors slammed shut in fear that the gipsy will charge
too much for its fortune.

The hours tick, I watch the fingers become day — then two: the
weeks have finished themselves, months turned to years. Time has
washed itself of our little years, our years of loving.

12

So on the cultured signal
And soft on the silver shoe
That shows itself unwilling
To dance, to dance, to rue.
Slowly the curls are wound
And wild the grease is smeared
Over the old pathways that should not be neared.

Can you leave the mouth alone
As you never know what to do
And when you come to the teeth,
My love can you polish them anew?
Should the account be paid —
It's been posted often enough
— Or left to lie on the shelf
And fob the collector off?

Tell me if he's young
And tell me if he's true
Or if he's got my stamp,
Or does he like the aspen tree by the yellow lamp?
Now give me the beauty patch
And I shall show the way
To tread in the tarnished slipper
To dance, to dance, to pay.

April 1952.

13

I shall sing you many songs
And with them many lies — to the eyes,
        to the eyes of the pale blue skies.
And you shall know the hurl, its break with the pearl
        in the shell, in the shell in the deep sea well
Where no feathers flay and the sponges play
        in the sheam of the seam of the cave I say,
Go away, go away,
Yet come another day.

Where the sea lies still, and the foam bemoan
Then trembles down alone, to the bed,
To the deep sea bed,
Where the fishes play.

4.40 p.m., 7th June 1984.

14

The raindrops fall in all seasons
Their beautiful colours light the horizons of our seeing,
            or should do so.
The earth is awakening yet again,
Morning kisses our brow.
Oh you noble and brave winged marvels,
The storms, the tempests do not discourage you. You birds, it
            seems to me, have more courage than us. You do not seem to
            lose your destiny or your faith in your return to your home
            suns.

11.10 a.m., 15th June 1984.

15

Bird fountain, deep fountain: fountain cold as well: fountain
without love — the birds fly to you from the world's four corners,
playing unnoticingly that you do not love them. They are quite
unaware in their noble innocence that the present blue light skies
which light their plumage will, like the world and its children,
forget the message for example that the dove has always tried to
bring us; and, like children shouting unminded in their silly and
oft cruel games — I have seen a charming little girl jump joyfully
on top of a pigeon in a London park and kill it quite slowly, then
run away screaming in pleasure wanting an ice cream — throw stones
at these frail creatures of peace and sometimes hit them, and the
world unminding unminds. Children, you have no right whatsoever
to kill.

Fountain of birds, fountain dismantled because we have thrown in
too much litter, bitter as death that you can no longer flow
because of our havoc to you. Your waters were poisoned by our
thrown-out stubs and cigarette boxes. You are demented as you are
being destroyed by us.

180

16

Why do you birds disappear, why do you not remain faithful to us?
Some of us do not kill you, and some of us have halls of hope as
beautiful as yours. In the right deep centre of the green leaves
and branches, the songs of swallows and in their season nightingales
linger in our memories.

I do not think the metamorphosis between us quite impossible.

I only wish for joy from that which brings me sadness. I have
worshipped a single rose which was hardly visible in the near dark
twilight just remaining, and nearly listened to its scent.

Fountains of dreams where memories die and torment the colours of
the beautiful world and the beautiful people — fable of flowers'
empurpled lives do not exist for us, those of us who can see
behind deceit. But if the birds can still bless us and forgive
our conceits; but if the beasts which we cage and hurt can
forgive us as well, and somehow arrive at a perfect harmony and
acceptance of our follies — at this moment of time, I must remain
silent.

The Capitol of Pain

4.40 p.m., September 9th 1984.

1

The year could have been a joyful one,
A summer of beauty. Are we two still alone I wonder?
And the winter, the snow covering all the seeing landscape
    like a tidily made bed.
Then the springtime which seems totally detached
    like a king bird with its wings strong, new and confident,
    so well formed.
Return of death, return of life. I pass through the seasons'
    days and glooms by a gossamer mirror which leads straight to
    the centre of my heart and nature of sorrow.
Woods slaughtered by green sunlight blood, savage, and confused;
    faithful, well instructed in its functions, unalterable
    yet ever changing in its time and functions but always
    discreet, unpardoning man in his slaughtering madness,
Like a solitary woman who has designed a beautiful dress,
    suddenly to be transported to the deserts of despair and
    knowing that her despair will never vanish there.
The sun born again shines on a part of me
The moon born again shines on my open hands which resemble blind
    eyes searching for the limits of the stars —
But even the moon has its limits of healing me.

2

The truth is that I have never learnt not to love
    and the truth is that I love.
By day each day love holds me more, first and foremost.
There are no regrets for yesterday — I forget, or try to forget
    them, but I make no progress.

And love has not the time to fix, but design patterns in the
    ever moving sand, licked by the great tongues of the wind.
I speak in and on the air. I speak and cry in despair,
    and understand that I must because I am there.
The shades and the mouth breathing softly into the azure blessings
    of night's darks and comforts — oh sad things which we do
    for a little smile or comfort or for a tender look. To
    shout just for the love to return itself to itself and
    pretend that the voice belongs to someone else is some
    comfort.
Nothing can disarrange light's order,
Nothing can disarrange my being my sad me,
And those whom I love are there on life's table
    that can be thrown and cleared away so quickly.

9.32 p.m.

3

I am my mother, I am my child
    and in each point eternal my mind becomes more clear.
My heart becomes sadder from what I see all around me.
I am my own sun: I am my own gladness in the night's nocturnes.
All these words agree —
    the mud is caressing when the winter unfreezingly
    finishes its bitterness with itself.
The sky is still brooding and subterranean because it has seen
    its own dying
The sky is not only for morning and daytime after a day of sorrow
But man — man with lazy steps to save or help or heal.
Man with eyes of glass and cold seas, kills hope in many of us
    in the voice of reason. Mortal man devises his own lies
    and pretends he will never die, divests himself of all
    blame, and when he is frightened screams — It is not me,
    it is not me who caused this evil thing to be.

4

From the ocean, from the river's sources,
From the mountains and fields spring will-o-wisp phantoms of life
    with their sordid shadows of death.

183

But between us, in the night's first living there is an ardent
    and precise love which puts all things in this earth right —
    intact, even leading in daytime time incarnate in all living
    and our knowing. All this knowing though is enough to hang
    or kill all loving.
The seas our union, fire our eyes for all other lives living
    to recognise in us our brief encounter in our very finite time.
One heart alone is simply not a heart.
One single heart means all hearts
And our spirits' stars fall upward to the sky stars
    in the light time of regards.
Our small light for a time paints the land with hope.
A man singing of all the human plagues for you the living which I
    love, and for all other hearts which we in turn return love
    by loving. Those who have never envied things or other
    people will help me finish all my giving. Nothing for
    yesterday, nothing for yesterday to forgive.

1 p.m., 12th September 1984.

5

Oh my Demon Socrate.
Thoughts of a poet, thoughts of a mathematician, thoughts of a
    no one, thoughts of all and any subject.
Compare and taste, all these words which do not possess any hands
    or fingers on an angel or the Angel of Death. Simply
    thoughts, well done and let announced to and through the air.
    Here we shout foul words about things not understood. Shop
    poets, with their little lyres roughly carved in bad wood
    and poor painted gold, speaking in puerile verse repeated
    words meaning nothing but nothing.

1.30, 13th September 1984.

6

I have always needed someone to live for,
    to exult in and for others' good.
I am not a stone or a piece of wood,
My flesh is much too alive still.
Hands which join leading to life's dance

184

by wings and singing of the extraordinary birds,
   the fine proposition of the just words
Full of our pleasure book from which we learn the flight made
   in the immense skies,
   in the universal season of all time and the winds,
A sail resembling a vanishing dream.
I can live in the confines of four walls, but never in man's
   prisons — and I can never forget the out of walls, the fields
   of open land in all seasons.
Each one of us has to discover his good,
   which means living with all his shades as well.
It is not necessary to be each one to be all and sense the world's
   awful pain surrounding us,
To be wise without being mad
To be mad without knowing wisdom.

Come to me and walk beside me,
You who are alone, alone as I am.
I approach you, I who appear from out the crowd.
One caress, one lying side by side, one nakedness to forget our
   loneliness in this impossible life our universe,
Our love which has no aim, but is not indifferent to our pain.

3.29, 13th September 1984.

7

Looking towards you my quiet beautiful images,
My arms are always stretched towards your insatiable harbours.
Come, adventure that portends death.
Come quickly quickly, the night presses forward total,
You will perish without living and your ephemeral joys will
   never rejoin the sky's rose light time.
Have you never seen broken the last tender rose — the rose
   you most admired?
I can no longer shut out time or space, the hurt and bruised
   and the many flags of life and living. And this grand port,
   these mysterious arrivals of ourselves in time can no longer
   be borne. I must dismantle them all, foreteller of frozen
   hurts that feel this tender skin which I hide in will most
   surely break my flesh.

Close, close all offences and entrances, eyes which renounce the
    veritable night's pain. Accept with the mystery which
    surrounds it the strangeness of a sad birth and a maternity
    of dumbness with thoughts.

9 p.m., 14th September 1984.

8

This cruel bird the night long haunts me with her sleeplessness,
    sings her noises. It is impossible to think of her making
    all this sound, all this loud sound perhaps of an unquiet
    warning coming from this small small soft feathered thing,
    continuing until the burning time of a summer morning comes.
You pierce my heart and fix destiny for me, with such regard of
    hopelessness that I cannot reply to it.
The twilight is reborn again but I cannot forget your face in
    the passing minutes of time we shared between us a fine
    day or two which already no longer belongs to me. One more
    day is but a vain sadness for us perhaps.

9

Some stars shine like a dark piece of amber, some like onyx;
    others seem made from very clear sapphires. I think that
    God must have closed his eyes for some time now.

10 p.m., 14th September 1984.

10

Neither flowers nor wreaths, we say.
April is not of our mind,
She blinds the burying with her own beautiful colours.
April with her catafalques of tulips and other blooms
    has other things to do than mourn our dead.

1 a.m., 15th September 1984.

11

Man of night, I have lived in a destroyed world.
My words, my gestures seem to creep from ruin to ruin.

186

Totally alone, it seems now for many years, far from poems'
     songs in a wooded desert I find no comfort. And the poems
     which sometimes fall from me are fainter than the falling
     of dead leaves onto the soft emerald moss earth.

     12

Man that never held anyone by the hand
Man that never found anyone to love
Has already changed the future by his sufferings.
It was unfortunate that he could do nothing for the past,
     that he loved money. The social functions were very
     important to him.
So he stayed in the desert.

If anybody has stolen from you, then tell them 'These are still
     mine, why do you not steal them as well?'
If someone is strange and hurtful to you and causes harm, then
     you must ask him to do more, if you think that it will
     cure him of his violence towards the world. And if he wishes
     to destroy you, tell him that you wish to rebuild his spirit.
     He is in great darkness where darkness dwells, therefore he
     must be loved; for those in darkness have the most need of
     love and loving.

2 p.m., 17th September 1984.

     13

We at least were faithful. Oh encounters, our winged thoughts
     side by side flying seemingly into the earth and the
     improbable ever changing sky's lightning moods ever
     changing from black to rose.

But what is this seen unseen light which shines still more
     brightly over us? Is it the reflection of our dying
     audaciousness, we who dared life to stretch us fully? Yes,
     we like Ariel encircled the entire world and saw the beauty
     and saw the shock of the grating midden of men turned rotten
     with hate — we tried too much to help. But alas we could not
     do very much. A scratch, perhaps, nothing more.

We shall no longer try to interfere.
We will simply weep for you.

14

Our bones have touched the earth,
Our faces crumble. My love, nothing is ever finished.
A new loving which comes freshly to my heart in one cry only
       reminds me of our past loving. And if the warmth of our
       heart's feeling should be killed, even then, my love,
       our loving continues. Love is always opposed to dying —
       love is infinitely loving.
Our pains floating on rivers' life side along side with other
       pains as well cannot be forgotten, or must not be.
Death has not grown any larger throughout time, and mourning has
       always been the same all time everlasting.
The good joys which lie next in turn are surely there
       — fear not, life is not always angry.

15

Oh you great clouds and visible columns of light, play and sleep
       — our oppressors here on earth cannot touch you as they can
       and do touch us, we who travel in perilous times and strange
       seasons of this earth. Without doubt their poisons are
       strong and could easily affect us, we who eat and drink of
       their fatal concoctions. We even have to buy them because
       there is not much else to eat or drink to live by.

Play and sleep, play and sleep in spite of the oppressors if you can.

16

Where does the pain come from, neither the thrush nor the
       nightingale will tell me. Fading in the forgotten sadness,
       I forget the voice of all heart's torments. I dream
       meanwhile of my past vast summers, rose lit with the
       splendour of youth in the castle of youth, where youth itself
       was the coinage of the grand realms. I am lost if I cannot
       find the black secret of my torment. And in its turn the
       black column of night finds me, although I search a never
       ending path of pain. This sadness without any kind souvenirs
       haunts me.

Even when September and autumn finishes there is no end, but a
    beginning of winter for me.
And outside my mind and heart I remember your loving, as good
    as an old French song and fresh bread.
My sadness is recognised at last — it is the heart's
    assurance which saddens me, and that refrain, like a naked
    footfall, troubles the green waters of silence.

17

The wind is much stronger now. A lamp is less obscure.
We must find the halting place where the wind cries 'Pass'
    through me. Then we shall know that it is impossible to do
    impossible things, such as making mirrors disappear.
Oh earth become tender, oh branches ripen my joy!
The complete sky looks ghost white, so white.
My downfall my love,
My terrible pain and joy.

12.35, 25th September 1984.

18

And in the sacred troubles of remorse, all the pleasures that were
    felt and got became worthless mountains of abuse. Summers of
    power, the logo of all the world, hope and home of man's
    last resources, come alive together. There is nothing
    lasting or growing for anyone not giving — you sower of
    seeds, you maker of powders that some women put on their
    faces to make time sleep for them for a little while —
    although sleep is already breaking in and awaking you. This
    déjà vu whispering to your heart and mind plays and replays
    this strange music of the past, which you belonged to. All
    flowers of summer that I capture in my hands and arms
    stripped and captive, culled for a time, making my hands
    tremble because they are beautiful: this round of colours,
    making words signposts of new meaning for us all if we
    understand, explains the infinite, explains the firmaments,
    explains the rapport of value and no value, explains the
    perfumes and memories of things past, explains what makes
    white paper and black print sing loud to us; explains what

makes leaves light and brittle in autumn's colding
sunlight; explains the branches' supplications to the
gods.

Let us render to all light a tribute of justice, making immobile
the centre of all man's hopes and horrors. One can still
see the hope and glory of the young. My friends, do not
turn against the young or laugh at their hopes. My friends,
do not fail to help the old in their time of hopelessness
and disillusion. My friends, remember that if you do these
foolish things you are only killing yourselves. And that is
the end of my song today.

2.39 p.m. 25th September, 1984.
Zurich.

19

('In a village looking by the water and seeing some mountains')

I no longer desire to see your face open to me, or hear the
comforting waters of the stream remind me of your profound
eyes. To make me joyous, sad or tender, my closed pathways
of pain must only live in these words and my tears must dry
away. Wells of memory, will you never stop making me drink
of your bitter springs?

Let your anger sleep and melt away the storm clouds of your
domain.
Poet, forceful and confident, be joyful again, though you doubt.
Even though I shall never stop climbing your perilous cliffs
and surely fall away.

To Fly Away from Peril

18th October 1984.

Snows of snow, and in the snow of snows there was a child who
threw out in hope his soul and heart to him once, but he did
not notice anything. And as he passed, he closed his eyes,
and as though he were blind and deaf he heard nothing and
saw nothing.

Once a man and a woman passed — once, once, one day, the long
pathway, holding hands to keep warm, and they did not see
or hear anything either.

The heat and the cold are there, they have their uses — but not
for me, for I am locked up like a fly in amber.

The image of she whom I loved, reflected in the waters of memory —
one time, one time, the waters clear and pale, I saw all
times reflected there where the damp wood lilies grow, in
their sad knowing that we shall live and die in this soiled
world.

The lace caps of the mountains cannot help us, nor can the seas
with their ever moving returns, nor the rose flowers' scents
help us — only remind us of our lost hopes in the land of
desolation where we sit and see the snows of pain. The birds
flying in the southern damp fogs leading to desolation in
the land of desolation, they fly with wet wings and hang
heavily in the air, these birds. It is a bad day for them,
a day some of them will not return from. But they continue
to fly, these creatures, some white, some black — these
beasts, these birds belonging to our land, the lair of hurt
and decay. And these birds, busy with their work as I am
with mine, talk of loving, talk of pain, talk of never doing
wrong or this or that again. But in our fate, both they

and we repeat all our doings in the land of despair; and
in our memories of silence, we sorrow.

In the first garden do flowers grow, the lilies and fruits,
the earth has forgotten the winter time.

The sky and grass are painted with childhood's blues and
greens — as they should be.

In the full haze of summer, to sleep in grasses and forget Latin
seemed quite right — and right it was for that time.
Oh Finisterre, you strange part of France that made me part
of you, I did not know that summer would not last me my
very lifetime then. Autumn came, and then the winter of my
innocence made me long for my soon to be violets. Seasons
of my days, seasons of my loving — that I will not be able
to forget or forgive.

The Hawk tears himself into sand, you see, you turn away. That
he is very high in his domain, his sky where there is no
shadow to hurt him. But as he is suffering the seawreck
of his dying, he still sings, he still flies but crying
his bird call of death when he knows that he is falling
to the dying land. The Hawk called me and I accepted
his cry. I accepted to live for him in my world — bad,
miserable, I accepted, but I misguided him otherwise, I
did not listen to the dead words of the dead that kept
repeating their warnings that man brings destruction and
ruin. And I made my vain words obey my vanity, turning lies
to truths. All these were lies to ensnare him from his
skies. These words seemed clear and true to him because
he trusted in my eyes. So the bird sang his songs
trustingly, and thought the earth and man beautiful. I am
no siren, but I sang a siren's song: and I detest myself
for this action, the cold mirror of deceit — bringing me
long years of silence in the night. Later on I heard him
sing again — but this time, not for me the sleeper and
keeper of nothing. The Phoenix bird with all his triumphs
triumphs over me, and the only death which I must mourn
is man's, in his sad eternity of lies.

His voice full of ironies in the pure and distant trees lives in

192

his never death, telling us, telling me, that our hopes
are hopeless, bound in our own busy sounds of ourselves.
I fear that our harbour will be of blackened glass
through which we shall not pass. Will it be like ploughing
the rocklike earth? When we sense that the plough has
found the very centre of the ungiving earth and its secrets
in the shadows which are torn up from the dark, we invite
death and kill the soil as we kill all things. In the
trees, in their flames and fruits, from time to time, the
fine rapiers of blue and red light tempt us to our
forbidden paths, and following them is like opening
Pandora's Box. In the black night all the pus and filth
of wickedness seeps out unnoticed — till light time comes.
The wish to live here in this hard land is so dear to me
that I would willingly close up myself and be taken into the
ever closing forests which I now belong to.

It is in the earth, on and in it, that we must live — we have no
time to waste away. The shadows shall soon be shades. Here
is all the light which I can give you. Here is all the truth
I know, and though in exile I will still tell you that love
is all I know. Sentinels standing along the avenues of dark
fly into the profound skies. Birds, we kill you, and only
the trees mourn your loss. In the patterns of time, of sad
time, Phoenix, from the wooden embers of the fire which I
have lit, let me see you and your joy again.

Is it because I have chosen liberty that I have become a captive
to the concepts of freedom that irresistibly tie me to my
past and present being?

The child that shows you the path quickly and kindly,
unknowing that he has been kind, remains with me all my
years because he did show me love, and in the language
of the unfelt kiss and kisses of the mind, teaches you by
strange means the magic of the mind that sometimes shines
from his eyes. We walk in the breeze and gales of the
world's roads and footpaths. A walking stick to measure
the infinite does not help us at all, or prepare us for
infinity.

'Car j'ai de grands departs inassouvis en moi'

R.R. Autumn 1942.

I have wondered sometimes whether eternity might not after all exist as the endless prolongation of the moment of death, and that was the moment that I would have chosen, that I would still choose if the people whom I loved were living; and thankfully I still know about loving those that are still living now. The moment of absolute trust and absolute joy, the moment when it was impossible to quarrel because my loving made thinking an impossibility of doing so.

I am standing, and patience all gone. I walk along the streets, not daring to move too far lest I should miss you, apprehension and the autumn time making me cold. My companions in my waiting are with me as memories. It was for you, when it's said and done, that I waited. You that I have waited for, am waiting for, I have waited so long and searched for everywhere in my thoughts and my dreams.

You have come after all. We sit down in a small cafe, drinking. You talk away simply to bide your time and to say that we cannot continue like this any longer. But I love you. I wish that I could jump away from this world because I am so sick of it, and I think of the seas of escape, but there is no escaping love, so that there is no single thing that the eyes see in this world that does not remind me of my loving and the people whom I have loved. Everything flows in the great river over the devastated lands which thirst hungrily for the water and the waterfalls of thanks that deafen all my doubts. Not all the poisonous springs of blood that I have hurt can take my tides of love from me. And I go through the everyday actions, but my mind is drenched with all the tiresome intercourse of everyday living, and I do so hate it. There seems no escape for me, and I am like an idiot crying out my eyes, for I am taken up with feeling and have no choice in the matter. I am taken by sorrow, but I cannot help the sorrows of the world. No, I cannot escape myself even.

The clock is wound up and starts to register fractions. Time cannot be stopped for you or for any other people, who will some day look at you unseeingly because they do not think your grief or mine is theirs. They suppose that they will escape all the sadness, and that the foul stench of the world is not for them; and so the clouds pass on. Your secrets are quite safe until you tell the world it is doomed, and that no one will escape. They will all die. Yes, I know you, for I am part of you, as much as I am part of myself. Possessions are daydreams, and soon they all are swept away by time. You see they never belong to any of us. There is only a part of myself that I can give. You took my eyes and saw things which I could never see for myself. I made from words a strong cord that could attach the moon to the sea, wrestling with the everlasting tides of man.

O for the wide strength that you gave me, to transplant the desert and make cool earth from the brittle sand grains. Let the night complete itself out of the wilderness, and turn the horrid noise which taunts us wherever we go into silence.

The road was long, and the light that travelled along it made me blink to stop dazzling my eyes. It was night-time, and I was very unsure, so I looked past all disturbance of the world, or so it seemed then, for I was young. Across the road I saw the kerbstone and your companionship. All activity stopped. We were marking time. The boat rocked, the wind blew into its sails, and our journey had started. Then the link broke. I crossed back to the other side of the road. The clocks turned, and soon the lamps were grey in the still dark night. When you said goodbye it was late. I am myself, I know that I belong alone. You took a compass and got away from shallow waters. We shall see and feel the world around us. For my part, in grief, I start collecting forgotten tales and songs that were old a thousand times past. But as you told them they became new, for I had not heard any one of them before, because I had never heard them spoken in your voice.

We said farewell, and I said: 'Can I see you again?' The telegraph poles leap away. The wires undulate, forming soft curves from the top to the centre, then back again. It was a mistake to suppose that I would not travel any more. In the railway carriages I look into the already dead faces of people who are dried up, and their cold eyes stare back at me. I grow tired, and I dream of woods and the flowers and the waters that fly across space, my space. The wires sing their new burden very slowly. The pendulum cuts the edges of the moon, and the white fuel lights the country of the sky, and the star columns which are so slender, and the night-time is miraculously silent. Through the waking days that followed I wanted to sleep and dream of reassurance. The woods passed; the flowers and the waters, like vast bird shadows, fled across space. I walked by the glass river that mirrored your face until I broke the surface with a stone. My eyes were blind, and my fingers cut themselves in the ragged and sharp hurt of memory in the dusty wastes of the world. Oh let the gods give me back my eyes so that I may be able to look. Tomorrow, tomorrow might help me, but what of strength? Is it enough that I can endure this pain? Sufficient for ever, you said, but now you disremember and abuse as though you had never understood what you were saying or what I have tried to give you. You must keep, even if only in remembrance, some of my love. There are plenty of tomorrows, and there is always the wilderness of the soul. All is a dream, I tell you. There is nothing to understand when everything is said and done. Perhaps out of dreams there is some kind of loving, but love has, it seems, to live in unfurnished houses with doors slammed shut in preconceived fear, and the gipsy will tell your fortune but charge too much, watching the finger of time become present, past and future. The years grow up. Time is always watching and ridding itself of the little years which close themselves for ever.

F.B. 1951.

The waters of love flood everything, so that there is really nothing that our eyes see that is not covered in. There is no angle that the world takes with the lovesight in my eyes that is not a symbol of love to hurt me. The precise shape and the fine geometry of his hands as I look upon them dissolves the mind and the spirit into water which flows away in love's torrent of pain. All that starts, all that has beginning must oh so surely have an ending. How can I go through the necessary actions of the days when so intense a fusion turns the world into vast seas of despair. I am possessed by love, and it seems that for me there is not another option. There are no mountains of myrrh, and no hills of Christ's frankincense for me. You, my dearest, are in another country. Oh where is my country? Shall I have lived to taste the salt waters of my sadness which I am poor enough in spirit to grudge? I do not wish to blaspheme, or think, and say 'See what I am in hurt from!' Remember also that I said 'I know, this is all there is.' The words return to the barren silence, stripped of kind fragments, like the hands and tools of a dexterous surgeon who conquers and cuts the taut springs of that which binds us together. Their anonymous blade thrusts into my shell, and my soul is withered and seeks escape into the memory. So now I say, not for sense, nor greed, not pity, nor any worldly wisdom, or any sense

196

of duty did I give my hand in companionship and love to you. It seemed the only inevitable and the only possible action to do on my part. Know that I said also, 'Though this is all there is of me, it is the vulnerable mortal person, and can so simply be attacked, so that my poverty-stricken message against the highly financed and suspect world is not enough.' I wonder though where I lost myself in my loving. I know I must accept it without despair, that hope of tomorrow must be enough. I am without any flowers of promise. Is love stronger than death? After this question, why should I so paradoxically give incidentals of delight — and why now, when not to have known love, when my mother's clutched hand held me with claws of love and misplaced pity, when there was too much taste of hell. Alas these thoughts are my sins, my garments of shame. There are some who love Lucifer, simply because he lost the battle of God, though I feel the Devil has a portion of justice on his side and perhaps there was something rotten in heaven. I have seen gnawed animals caught, fixed in the steel teeth of the trap. Is heaven like that, I wonder?

I acknowlege all the meaning we found together, and the time we sought to arrange in ordered places ourselves to ourselves. We decided everything, and polished some principles so very well. 'Fate takes me on my journey; I know not where I go.'

You went away, and some little time after, I saw you. You smiled. I was walking with you again, and that was sufficient.

The night sleeps, and I visit all sections, the small cracks and the corners of my mind. Time sways, the night eyes are watchful of the dawn which comes in pale shafts of light breaking darkness slowly.

There is no answer. The hours close, the bubble shall crack and die, there will be a new pattern; and my cry shall bury itself in the earth in wait for new seasons of sadness to grow again for all of us. The wind is lazy, it barely touches my face. Then all changes, there is joy.

I am falling through the filter system of the world as I die, oh where is my fair world?

Collected Poems
Volume 5 1986

17.36, 24th March 1986.

Mountains of grand abuses,
The summit of your great pride
The last great charity.

Nothing but void and avalanche
Nothing but distress and regret!

All those troublesome troubadours
who saw that, in one fine summer
their songs were lies. Damn them!

Inexorable shows of love that
torment us no longer, now
that the sable's silken summer is over.

12th April 1986. 12.17 p.m.

I have never written poems without you
It is as though I were plunged into a cold stream
of sadness — my Gethsemene, if you like.
Christ was always alone with his doubts and sorrows.
I receive the present time as though it were a
treasure of bronze loving Autumn. All my songs were
sung in the time and hope of youth.
My joy now is knowing that sometimes I was
able to love quite well.
The masque of smoke, the blue Debussy woods burn
the leaves and turn them into invisibility
My grand black star you grow in and upon me
you have nearly encircled that part of my domain
which I call my heart.

You, my vision have blinded me,
The echoes of lies rub themselves out to annul
my past kisses.
My love we sleep together
and we have laughed in youth's morning time
You were my eternity when we lived side by side
Oh profound sleep, that is the order of innocence
to live higher than our dreams that was our
pleasure in a new world always just a little bit
too young at that moment of time for us. Could we
have forseen our winter?
No matter, we were free and we have known
joy.

13th April 1986. 03.07 a.m.

I search for a false semblance of loving
An avenue that is so much larger
than my heart and mind
A smile that would melt stone to honey
and a kiss that would calm mad dogs.

My body is nothing but my own and not fit
for much other than for my trying to keep
away from the HYENAS of this world
so that it will not be torn to shreds.

I must travel into the light
there are no shadows in the darkest dark
until I sink into the uttermost pit.
Death will take my substance and my shadows.

Tears will warm my face
I walk towards the sunlight which is rising from
the blackened horison.
Already I am making provisions against my forgetting.

Moon and Sun are you one?
I see and I feel the Sun
But, already the musk of dark comes to me.
I see, because I am free to see.

In spite of dark spirits
I made a grand journey
into the greenest of countrysides.
Nature, is, it seemed to me to be giving birth.
I became summer out of despair
Legions of birds opened their peacock feathers
and gave me all of their songs in their
summer time.

The waves of morning lifted them up
one by one and they flew back into their journeys;
The flowers shared their colours with me.
At those times who could not wonder at wonders?

13th April 1986. 11.00 a.m.

The night and its army columns of dark
vex us when all is done, we are blind now,
we have travelled in light, we thought in light
we saw. Now our paperchase markings
cannot help us.

In time that resembles a death
we play a tragedy of living
A game that traps us, A game that hurts us
and makes us block our pain.

I miss the hurt of understanding,
that at least was faithful
in this ancient world where I am told I belong.
It is a pity that my heart and mind are not kind.

13th April 1986. 1.40 p.m.

I watch with surprise the eternity of sunrise
Ruins of loving; the world tolls for its dead.
Turn the time to zero
my good path of springtime,
open the earth tenderly
Love which is fertile laughs at age
and welcomes all tomorrow's lovers

200

Joy is essential, they sing of hope,
they have won!

There were times when he felt calm, in command;
others, when the wings of fear were dreadful
in him, telling him to give up hope
But this he would never do, he would have
to concentrate minutes at a time until, rather like
slotting transparencies in a viewfinder he
would be able to find the right picture.
The river seemed the colour of ice and the sky
had forgotten to wash itself. It touched
him as he observed that nature herself was
in an untidy mood that day. As
unprepared for an unexpected visit as he
had been unprepared by the discovery of
what had lain deeply buried within himself.

11.37, 25th April 1986.

The thousand trades that are in essence all the same
All the streams flow together are the same
Bands of wild dogs travel together, in spite of
our chains to tie them because we are afraid of them.
Our quivering fright cannot hold the beasts of
power for good or bad.

The drops of rain pour down upon us in all
seasons, amid the great Horizons the earth
is shrouded in fear and the earth's morning
no longer bathes our tomented brows.

Each woman is unwinding her binding sheet
of death for us to catch in our despair
after all they bore us, those women, in hope
they are the incendie to our pleasure.

Dove, you noble bird, let the storm pass over us.

1

Beauty that is best remembered in echoes
Aubades best remembered in the trellisses of
the woodland's days of winter
Youth best remembered in and for its unknowing wisdom
Lovers and the best beloved ones no longer
able not to love.

Truth is the candle flame in the darkened room
that we live in. In my country
there are no rooms for your vain branches of pride
In my country we try to give thanks.

2

Those whom have loved me and then grew
to dislike and then forget
Seem to start searching for me anew
Some cried at our new meeting
Some, though very few were pleased.

3

My sister cold, like the cold grass of winter
As you walked away I saw you grow
higher, oh so much higher than your
enemies.
Greener than my souvenirs.

4

You are the light, you are the night
This lantern is for you to see with
This wooded board is for your sleep
This water for your thirst
These walls are supposed to imprison you.

1

What better thing to arrange
If not our death?
I had been afraid
Because I have not done very much.
Not enough truth to stop the
Corroding lies which shatter us.

Thus I looked for the truth of my words
and found only pathways and signposts
It is impossible to fight any longer our foolishness
and our deceits.
The fires are dead, I no longer sleep.

2

Look, all the tracks, all the pathways
you should follow are closed to you
you have no tickets left, no receipts
for work done

Your footsteps make no noise
they break no twigs or burnished
copper leaf paths, because you dare not move.
And you, you deep shades who are you,
what are you?

Days dropping into night.

3

You are already separated from yourself
The same cry of hurt sounds alarms
but you do not hear them.
Your own anguish and pride
turns away the tides of other's pain
You are already lost!
Your mind and heart where are they?

4

For you I shall light a fire that
will burn night out.
For you I shall gather up the four winds
to stop their shouting rages.
And lift up horizons of dark doubt which
troubles darkness.

The stars shall never fall
promise me that you will not be afraid!

Collected Poems
Volume 6 1993

the time is 9.17 p.m.

1

Your footsteps, infants of my silence,
Sentiments which are placed in strange places
that led towards the repose of vigilances
There is no one left in the shade of divine silence
Do not haste to forget the act of your tenderness.

1993.

for Francis Baumli

Shura Gehrman

2

In the heart of night you and I, not Queen and King
In the heart, in the heart of the night
At this time your mouth is mine
    and mine is yours
We are a single joy in white dread of night.

3

Roses, you offend, the hurt you give grieves,
Offends because your beauty can be
    bought by anyone.
Your blushes are your lies,
Your fragrance never dies because
it becomes a clear echo of silence.
The shop-bought flowers shout out
Their mocking laughter of lies.

4

What are you doing all hours?
What do you wish for?
Do not press too much for realisation
The speed of destruction is too soon with us.
The disgust that kills us in the night has
found you and is always there.
I shall try to meet death standing can you
understand why and help me.

Tod 23 years old

5

I know that you are dying there,
deep in sorrow.
Your young bones shout hurt and decay,
Lamps and machines have no songs
or words to comfort you or help.
You have been made bald again my friend.
No amputation to extend your
twenty-three years, and you have left us now.
Your mother moans and grieves
and plants your grave with flowers.

1993.

The hourglass of silence has no grief.

My song is made my song is sung
It tells you what you know
That we are wrong.
wrong to move towards delight
wrong to look for pleasure
wrong to live with 'I'm All right'
cliches falling from our throats
in nearly every utterance,
in the bleak despair of fright
to displease anyone or anything
that might affect our money's fight.
For money is really our delight

forget yourself in sex or food or
any other indulgence which might
draw us to delight.

Never say I love you, it's not done
never touch anyone, you must understand
you must assume the bitter silence
lest those who know you, those who
love you should take fright. For love's
a slowly growing thing if it be love.

12th February 1993.

This for me is the only possible
path for me to follow in the everlasting
search for the forlorn task of understanding.
Sounds, the poem, try as I like, it's
always impossible. Do turn it off
whenever you like, it is after all
preparation.

There are toads and hacks which I shall
name that have shown their meanness of
spirit, heart and mind, their simple sillyness
and vulgar ignorance of the great Romantic
18th. and 17th. century. That perhaps have spent a few
years of their lives listening to
the poor and ordinary and simply proficient
that have attacked me in the poorest way
which they have at their disposition.

I am left alone with sighing
and this sighing is a goodbye
because it would take me into a language
of infinity and desire which in turn takes
me into delusion.

The Hopi, an Indian tribe, have a
language as sophisticated as ours but
no tense for past, present and future.
The division does not exist.
What does this say about time? Matter

207

that thing the most solid and well known,
which you are holding in your hands
and which makes up your body, is now
known to be mostly empty space. Empty space
and points of light. What does this say about
the reality of the world?

Mine!

To think that anything belongs to anyone,
is me for example is utterly foolish
as well as being downright wrong!

March 1993.

      To recognise
The terrible shock of love and loving
for the first time in a life is rather
like being in the full thrust and hurt
of a hurricane.

New Poems Old Thoughts 1993

1

Your footsteps of my silence
And my thoughts falling into place,
Like gossamers of the unheard spider's web
only seen in the frost day air of space.
No one, even you divine threads of my childhood
Can prepare me for these moments of the great memories,
Because my heart has lived into the land
of your golden footsteps
and cannot forget your eyes.

2

Present or absent the solitude
of very early mist covered rivers
Leading to the road of vagabondage
Enchaining the shadows of my mind
Like golden darts of pleasure that melt
Quickly when the remembered joy of our
loving comes, when the sky became
the cherished colours of our past days
secrets in the lost thoughts and soul of
remembered flowers of our gone ways
like newborn dreams.
Stay, oh you adored love of all my days
your repose enchants me with longing,
and invincible acclaim.

3

The skylarks of the night fly
as best they may and in their

silent solitude know that they must
shun the light. They are ghosts
in their soft sadness of mortal loss
they know not how to grieve or cry.
In the ruins of lost dreams
all pleasure is unchanged
and sadness annulled for the
skylarks of the night.
The moonlight is their lantern
which shines upon the earth rooted trees
that cannot give them infinite light
nor man infinite love.

4

Day after day man changes blood.
There are no mysterious doors which
can alter through their portals
or change the seasons of his kind
to renew his childhood's light of love nor
the sadness of his maternal love
or any lust which oppose it may break
his bondage.

Day after day man must face his
sad fate, and await himself in the
shadows of time.

5

Nature will always lean toward rebirth.
The waves of morning light change one
by one from night into the noosphere of light
and in spite of all ill will fight the dark
desires of man.

The fruits of my garden which flower and
grow in light delights me, and I am able
to wash my singing blood. There are
no lamentations here, the grace of your
kisses brings forth my childness and
the manhood in my heart and soul grows.

I can bear the possible deceptions of the future
in this manner, this rainbow manner of delight,
all of delight.

6

To see the minds of men and women
enshrined by rotten halos of delight.
Colours too bright which open your
eyes in surprise like prisms of
music formidably stopped and held
Colours that are of desire and fear
of softness and joy for the coming years
and the lives that vomit through your eyes
Colours that batter of despair that in
daytime sing out of beauty that are nowhere
One side of my heart is made to live there
the other side is the existence of your hopeful
joy like unknown magic of eternal life
in your cleverness of knowing your
victorious right.

7

I have long thought of life as an autumn mist
flowing out from the rivers which themselves
flow down mountain streams quite lonely

Beasts kill for food,
Men kill for their coarse blood lust.

Talk to me they ask, and answer the riddle
of who I am. A voice replies 'love
and the safe conduct of your life
until you reach the portals of your death,
you the hunter that has killed so often
find dying now awesome for yourself.'

You have danced your Quadrille of life
and your hand reaches but finds no comfort,
No angel appears to play the role of Saviour,
Cry out to the skies for there is beauty there
but you were not content to let the birds fly.

The silence is complete now and no one
heeds your cry. Do you envy the invisible
power promising you nothing?

Do you now understand the laws of sufferance?
You hear me cry for love
But love is a mystic power that for many
does not arrive.

8

Days of joy, days of rain
days of mirrors which are broken in pain
days of eyelids tightly closed to all Horrors
Hours that resemble days of captivity.

My heart still shines on Autumn leaves
and the flowers comfort me like a lover.
We have time yet to say our goodbye
and to contemplate thanking sky stars for our destiny.

I have looked in your most beautiful eyes
of gold, of silver blooms and sad as Brione
veritable gods, to me, Eagles of life
and lilies of the earth reflected shining into waters mirror

My life is sustained by life and death;
Devoured by the sounds of the seas and
the rivers running their remembering ways
Oh you birds of liberty and proud plumage
sing to me.

9

Your eyes are globes of light
flowers of dark anemones
that pierce you naked loving
Flowers of transparence that lead
to all the paths of your thoughts
Annullment of needless words
you efface all other images of my mind
and astound love that ever before was
known to me and yet can never be forgotten.

212

10

This little blemish of day's first light
This fire of night resembles a frozen-headed serpent.
The sound of the wild beasts in all our human hearts
reminds us continually of our origins in the earth's slime.
In the damp and cold earth of our earthly minds
and the Sun and the moon pass us by uncaringly

The forests whisper to themselves their secrets
in nighttime dark, you touch their bark,
you try to understand their language but they remain silent.
The light flashes codes to them which we do not understand,
we are the unwelcome strangers that
kill them, in their land.

You look into the reproachful eyes of the owls who
stare at you and the rainfall drowns your eyes
into melting insanity of the crow black of
        your lifetimes ruins.
And winter comes to make you live and die again.

11

The broken mirror of lost minds and souls
Day of closed eyelids forbidding us to see
our horizons so capturing us from our hopes

And although I have seen the world's most
beautiful eyes, Gods of adamantine night
light the white flying invisible and unknown
skylarks of the night.

Their wings are mine and nothing exists
for me but their singing flight of love,
My thoughts and hopes are sustained
by them and by my death.

12

Morning of summer, morning of winter
Night of summer clear and bronze of thunder
making us aspire once again to implacable
and unknown knowing of the mind

White seasons of loving invisible of understanding
    delights,
deadening seasons balancing us sometimes
with youth and age.

13

We sing in the valley of stars and play parts
which we are given. Sometimes we sing in joy
though at other times our tunes are not
content with our destiny and this is our
mistake, our songs you see are so short.

14

Invisible workings of the mind
reminding for all our time
the things that make us remember
our living and our lives past
The times of hate and fear as well
are there and will be there for evertime.
The crystal re-seeing of our youth that
we do sometime sleepwalk through until the question is asked
of us the things we wish to do,
is it money? is [it] trying to make, or
remake ourselves again without
riding in the comfortable cars of fame?
which does kill the soul and mind bewitching
our youth with gleaming white five pound notes to gain?
Once a woman asked me this and broke my
night time walking life.
I do love her for that
although this question made me poor
changing all horizons which were then undreamed of
in my mind although I was always missing
that part of loving, but loving was the path I chose,
although the road was somewhat troubled
by anguish at times it now seems beautiful to me
and I regret it not a single jot.

15

I paint in times of sorrow the masks
made are mine, and make true joy cry

I write in troubled silly times and sub
culture claims the Alan Yentob pranks
as many models of perfection
and prescriptions of great television time
that is so silly. Lined faces answer useless
general knowledge to make them dimly shine
the questioners become sad in their silliness
and shame, But money, money, is their aim.

1993

The breaking waves
and sea's muscles as they contract
shout and scream the laws of infinity to me

My soul will meet this curve of fact
which I cull from my blame of loving.

In assault and waves of light I will
kill all walls of bad and corrupt
power like the receding lips of
water leaving the white sands and foam
of folly.

Pilgrimage to Nowhere

1

In the centre land of make believe
which we believe in.
In the absolute daydream of our
living, which we believe in.
In the centre of mind, there grow
lies, which we believe in.
In the absolute centre of measured things
which we believe in.
In the absolute knowledge of our follies
that we believe in — so we die.

2

All the day she watched him, and the next
day also; her vigil was only interrupted by
the necessities of her body functions. She
saw that he was dying. He had returned to
her, her prayers had been answered. She
now knew that she would rather he had
lived, continued to live, and this
he probably would have done if he had not
undertaken this fearful journey at her
request. She would never pray again;
for anything important, she thought.
Perhaps time would make her forget,
make her repeat her mistake. After all
most people do repeat their mistakes
throughout their lives.

216

3

Mind and soul look outward and sees
what it does not understand, desires that which
it cannot have. Heart is troubled and
afraid —
The turtle dove has gone, flown
or fallen from the Acanthus Tree which
looks but does not see, stands and does not move,
grows but has not desire other than to
feed itself. Man if he is wise rests
beneath the welcoming branches, is supported
by its trunk and sheltered by its leaves.
He, if he chooses, shares the life of the
tree without breaking his own living
in convenance of the prescribed fooling of the world.
You, my friend must close the window that
looks outward, begin to look inward upon
your true self, perhaps with luck, you will
sit in my garden and become your own
    meaning.

The theatre was empty, through a wall
the fat middle-aged manager was talking
to someone unseen. Out through the stage
door into another time, no
tarmac but mud and very dim lighting
which came from the wooden houses that
straggled along the road, along which a few
horses and carriages moved
slowly. It had been raining so everything
was polished to a very high gloss.
The young man got into his
motor car and drove slowly along the
road and at the end of it, he turned
left. He felt a slight shock, he had hit
the corner of a red house without
causing too much damage to it or
his car. Then he parked the car and
walked back into the past. There were

people that he'd recognised which he
very much wanted to meet.

The voice of autumn is heard now
always through the days that shine in
the mind — the summered days spell joy and
nothing unhappy can ever happen in
the sunshine. On a midsummer's day
the new prisoner had been put in a cage.
Not a cell — but a cage awaiting his true
imprisonment. The warders were doing
other duties — therefore his time was being
spent not unlike an imprisoned bird.
The cage was big enough.
His face was already broken in despair.

December 1993

Oh man lost in the middle of forests of life
Have you any idea how to escape
You are as taut as a harp string
In your sharp, sharp awareness of mysteries you do not understand
Of colours that you see and do not know
Of colours that are so bright
As bright as anything Duannye Rousseau painted
You arrange your affairs meticulously to no avail
You behave like a puritan and you anthropomorphize animals
To the rage and disgrace of their own sensitive beings
You are us

I demand the fabulous flowers that we could grow in paradise
Our paradise, not an eternal paradise

A fortune that is fabulous for the soul and the mind
A fortune without the sordid reality of making money
Alas we have to do this
Grey and poor is the odour of unwashed armpits
And malevolence of greedy, avaricious and envious people
You walk through the verger of epic horrors as a sleepwalker
In a jade-like forest and carpets of winter anemones
That you disregard, that are in mourning for the world

From time to time you fall on your knees
And you weep till your eyes nearly fall out and scream I am lost, I am lost
We are all lost

Damn the Popes, damn religion, damn principles — honour scruples
Scruples might be nearer to God

Epilogue

I have danced at the centre of miracles and a thousand suns have painted the earth for me and I have died and I have hurt with the glory of loving. Those sad fates which await us, do not be afraid of, they are but our fears, they are but our pride: I shall be wiped away as everyone is, to spin in the silent circles of truth.